Advance Praise for
Surviving the Survivors

"Told in a clear and readable manner, this memoir is a chronicle of success and persistence in the face of great adversity. Surviving the traumas inflicted by parents who were irreparably damaged by the Holocaust cannot have been easy. Klein is very brave to have made her story public, and she is to be commended for the research she did to fill in the history of the times and the history of her family."
—MARGARET L. KRIPKE, Professor Emerita, The University of Texas MD Anderson Cancer Center

"In her debut memoir, *Surviving the Survivors,* author Ruth Klein, with both tenderness and candor, delves deeply into her family's dark and horrifying past as victims of the Holocaust. Though some miraculously survive despite the unimaginable, like Klein, each must bear witness to the many who do not."
—SANDE BORITZ BERGER, author of *The Sweetness*

"In her engrossing memoir *Surviving the Survivors,* Ruth Klein paints an accurate yet heart-wrenching picture of what it is like to grow up with parents who were irreparably damaged by the Holocaust. While every second-generation (2G) Holocaust survivor's story is unique, there are threads of similarity that will leave other 2Gs, me included, nodding their heads in solidarity with Klein's experiences and behaviors. And her unfailingly positive outlook and drive to succeed will leave you cheering for her to the final word of her book."
—EMILY WANDERER COHEN, member of the Jewish Book Council and author of *From Generation to Generation: Healing Intergenerational Trauma Through Storytelling*

"I found this book very compelling; I read the entire book in one sitting—just could not put it down. It resonates with the history, feelings, and struggles of Holocaust survivors and the second generation. The highlight for me was the last chapter and its new character, ending this memoir as an affirmation of life."

—JOYCE LEVINE, Secretary, American Gatherings of Adult Children of the Holocaust Survivors; Former Secretary, National Survivors of the Holocaust; and President, Manhattan Chapter of Women Holocaust Survivors

"An engrossing, compelling story—it is profound, harrowing and intensely moving. This story needs to be told, it needs to be read, and it needs to be understood."

—GRANT ARTHUR GOCHIN, author of *Malice, Murder, and Manipulation*

SURVIVING

~ THE ~

SURVIVORS

a memoir

RUTH KLEIN

SHE WRITES PRESS

Published September 4, 2018
Printed in the United States of America
Print ISBN: 978-1-63152-471-4
E-ISBN: 978-1-63152-472-1
Library of Congress Control Number: 2018937060

For information, address:
She Writes Press
1563 Solano Ave #546
Berkeley, CA 94707

Interior design by Tabitha Lahr

She Writes Press is a division of SparkPoint Studio, LLC.

Names and identifying characteristics have been changed to protect the privacy of certain individuals.

In memory of Sarah

If I'm not for myself, who will be for me?

If not this way, how? If not now, when?

—Primo Levi

～ CONTENTS ～

FOREWORD

On a sunny fall afternoon some years ago, my wife, Ruth, and I were having our ritual weekend coffee hour (*kaffeestunde*, as she likes to call it) at La Madeleine, a café and bakery in Rice Village in Houston. We had been living and working in Houston since 1985. Ruth is a pianist and at the time was teaching piano in Southwest Houston. I am a scientist at MD Anderson Cancer Center, where I had been recruited from Indiana University in Bloomington to join the nascent basic science faculty. I met Ruth in Bloomington, and we fell in love and decided we wanted to spend our lives together.

In the midst of our coffee, pastry, and usual chitchat, Ruth looked me in the eye and said she wanted to talk to me about something really serious. An unexpected heart attack and the subsequent death of a friend of ours, who was about my age and in seemingly good health, had mentally unraveled her, triggering memories she had kept buried for years. His death and funeral sent her into deep, dark, clinical depression. In the two or three weeks after the funeral, she could do nothing except think about the death of loved ones and the consequences of irrevocable loss. She knew she was soon going to lose her older sister Sarah, who had been fighting two types of cancer for seven years and was now in a grueling battle with metastatic colon cancer. What if I died? She became terrified that I, too, would soon die. Aware of the mental state she was in, she had begun seeing a psychiatrist, who thought her condition was quite serious and recommended she immediately begin psychotherapy coupled with anti-depression medications.

Remarkably, this was all news to me. I hadn't noticed any big changes in her behavioral patterns in the many days since our friend's funeral. When listening to what she had to say on this Sunday afternoon, I was obviously concerned, but not completely surprised. Over the years and after countless discussions about her life as a second-generation child of Holocaust survivors, I had more than a sense that there was an awful lot going on in her head. Facts about her former life were released to me only in bits and pieces. I had a vague picture of that life, but not enough to appreciate fully what was undoubtedly a most unconventional upbringing with many disturbing features. I also was mildly aware of how the historical forces, which pulled Europe and its people apart in the 1930s and 1940s, strongly impacted the lives of second-generation children like Ruth. But as you will soon read, Ruth's upbringing was unique even taking these considerations into account.

In Sarah's last few months of life, she and Ruth talked about writing a memoir about their childhood. Sarah was insistent this would be a compelling story and urged Ruth to begin the project. Even as Sarah's condition worsened, she retained her optimism about getting well and thought she would then be able to add her own thoughts and contributions to the proposed book. Sadly, Sarah did not recover and Ruth was far too overwhelmed by her sister's death to think about a family memoir. Although she never stopped grieving over Sarah's death, Ruth quietly resolved to write her family's history, not just to fulfill her obligation to her sister, but also to learn more about how her life came to be what it is today. When she conveyed her thoughts to me, I encouraged her to begin the project and in fact was quite enthusiastic about it. A few weeks later, Ruth mentioned to her close friend Judi Shur that she was planning to write the story of her family as survivors and second-generation offspring of the Holocaust. Judi, who is trained as an attorney, had a longtime interest in creative writing and was intrigued by the idea of a memoir from a second-generation point of view. Ruth asked her friend if she could help, and a partnership was established. Judi assisted in historical research and helped format this story and photographs into a memoir of family history, which Ruth then finally wrote.

Nearly eleven years have elapsed since Sarah's untimely passing, and during that time the intensity and effort on researching, interviewing, selecting photography, writing drafts, and rewriting drafts has ebbed and flowed. What emerges is a raw, sometimes tragic, sometimes amusing, but always engaging story of a family burdened by the weight of external and internal circumstances over which the family's central players sometimes have control, but more often do not. The story tells of aristocratic Polish Jewish merchants and landowners, horrific refugee and concentration camps, endless displacement, and unimaginable suffering. The story then continues in America, on rebuilding broken lives in California, only to have them break down time and time again. Yet despite all of this, Ruth survives the survivors; indeed, she flourishes. Her journey includes an intense passion for the purity of music, focused on a single metaphorical and physical instrument—the piano—and with her family's story always close by, it follows Ruth through her amazing life.

—Bill Klein
February 15, 2017

INTRODUCTION

Both my parents were Polish Jews, enjoying lives of wealth and luxury before Hitler invaded their homeland in 1939. With the click of a trigger, they suddenly became prisoners and refugees trying to outrun the nightmare of their existence. I was the second born of my mother's four surviving children. After they were liberated, my parents returned to war-torn Poland and Europe, and awaited departure from the displaced persons camps in Germany to immigrate to the United States. Shell-shocked, starving, and impoverished, they were among the survivors.

This memoir describes what it was like growing up as a second-generation child of the Holocaust. Every survivor has his or her story, and each one is unique. Yet in some ways, the countless stories all have common elements. Some are woven into my personal accounts of who I was then and who I am now. Knowing that most of my relatives died at the hands of Nazi murderers gave me a keen appreciation for the value of life—that it shouldn't be squandered over the selfish and inhumane acts of others.

I am a survivor—my sister Sarah and I, and later Gazelle and Fred, were born and bred of survivors. My story may shock, sadden, or sustain you. But it's my story. Mine alone.

Ruth in Monterey Park, California, 1956, Photo by Mietek

Chapter 1

THE REPLACEMENT

Monterey Park, California: 1956

When I was nine years old, my father tried to commit suicide and murder my baby brother. I found them after I had got my younger sister ready for her bath and went to look for my brother. The door to my parents' bedroom was closed, and when I entered, I smelled gas coming from the 1950s-style gas heater. My father was lying on the bed with my brother next to him. They had plastic bags over their heads.

I stopped him. Ripping the bag off my brother and grabbing him away from my father, I got my sister and we ran to the neighbors' house to phone the police. I stopped him because it was my responsibility throughout childhood to feed and care for my twin siblings, a brother and sister who needed constant attention. It was also my job to impose some sort of sanity on our household, and to constrain my father's lunacy.

This wasn't the first time I called on our neighbors for help because of my father's psychotic behavior. But unlike the other times, when the police only issued a stern warning and left, this time they took my father away to the psychiatric ward of Los

Angeles County Hospital, where he was ineffectively treated with electroshock therapy. A week later he was home again, initiating a new cycle of terror and abuse that our family would endure for another decade.

Like an ocean swimmer battling an inescapable undertow, I struggled by the minute through childhood to keep my head above water, and was pulled each day into an endless, swirling vortex of drudgery and mental anguish that would have consumed most adults.

I wish I could tell you that this memory—of my father trying to take his life and that of his children—is my worst childhood remembrance. But it's not. Our lives of surviving the survivors were just beginning.

Baby Ruth, Photo by Mietek

Berlin: 1947

My mother pushed and groaned with every contraction, determined to bring a healthy child into the world. This baby, she insisted with every fiber of her body, would not die.

There were no delivery beds in the makeshift American Red Cross hospital, the basement of a bombed-out church in West Berlin that served thousands of refugees displaced by World War II. Sick and injured children, men, and women sprawled out on gritty sheets draped over warehouse pallets made of splintered wood slats, rising just inches above the hard-packed dirt floors. With the help of a female doctor, my mother exerted her strength for one last push, and gave birth to a baby girl.

She named me Ruth, after the biblical survivor of hardships, the friend and companion to others, the devotee to Judaism. It was February 20, and my sister Sarah, who had been born in a Russian camp while my mother was in hiding in Siberia, was three years old.

By 1945 the American Red Cross was providing aid in Germany in the form of food, clothing, and other goods shipped from less devastated countries in the European theater. In Berlin, hospitals such as the one in which I was born were hastily set up to meet the medical needs of the hordes of refugees and displaced persons arriving battered and shaken. As horrible as the hospitals were, their disorderly, overcrowded, and sparse conditions were an improvement for people who survived the war living in forests and in concentration camps, prisons, or labor camps for months and years.

Throughout her life, my mother spoke reverently of the luxury of giving birth in an actual building after the war. "Ruthie was delivered by a real doctor from Philadelphia," she used to tell people. "We had nothing. Yet a woman came all the way to Germany to help the European refugees."

Perhaps her praise for the doctor came from her own dreams to become a pediatrician, an ambition dashed to pieces when Hitler invaded her Polish homeland in September 1939. Or perhaps she was awed by the doctor's ability to keep me breathing, since I was born prematurely and weighed only three pounds. This was long before the days of neonatal incubators, and the survival of such a tiny infant was an extraordinary event even with the best medical care, much less under sordid conditions.

I also had black hair all over my face, and my upper lip was still attached to my nose, my tongue to my upper lip. The Philadelphia doctor told my mother in six weeks she could operate on me to correct the defects, but fortunately I eventually transformed into a normal-looking baby. In an effort to console my mother, who was distraught over my appearance, my father smuggled a terrier-mix puppy named Rex into the hospital under his trench coat. My mother loved dogs and was delighted to see the tiny puppy peeking out from my father's coat pocket. Even as a puppy, Rex had a job—to be stationed next to me and protect me from insult and injury. In the refugee camps it was common to place babies in carriages out-of-doors to give them fresh air, since the *lagers*, or sleeping quarters, were not conducive to health. My mother was comforted knowing that Rex was always there to serve as my dutiful shield when people passing by my baby carriage stopped to stare.

Sarah at bottom left, my mother and father at top left, two soldiers in Polish uniforms, and other unknown persons in Siberia

Ruth in baby carriage, Germany,
Photo by Mietek

Sarah and Ruth in DP Camp, 1947,
Photo by Mietek

Sarah, Daddy, and Rex in the
Berlin DP camp

I was part of the "survivor baby boom," so named because the world's highest birthrate at that time was found in these displaced persons camps, where those who had not perished felt an unconscious yet powerful Darwinian drive to replace family members killed during World War II.

As so many other babies in these camps, I was ordained at birth to be a substitute for family members who had been murdered by the Nazis. Throughout my childhood this became an eerie and oppressive burden to bear. Desperately wanting to please my parents and live up to their expectations, I would grow up to become a straight-A student and an accomplished musician. But it wasn't enough. I was doomed to fail as a surrogate for all they had lost.

City Terrace, California: 1951

The piano stood like a lone soldier in the middle of our meager living room. Sunlight from the dirt-smudged apartment window cast dust motes that swirled in the air and landed on the piano's smooth, polished surface. Sarah and I stood agape before it, unable to believe our eyes, afraid to touch it. Our apartment had no furniture other than a kitchen table and one treacherous secondhand bed. Our parents could barely afford to purchase food, much less furnishings. We were hungry and broke, a post-Holocaust refugee family living on public assistance in the United States of America.

Yet now we had a piano.

It was a miracle—albeit a miracle Daddy had no means to pay for. Even at the age of four, I knew this wonderful new instrument was an impulsive extravagance, although by then I had given up trying to understand why Daddy did the things he did.

My mother, Bronia, in 1948

Chapter 2

BRONIA AND MIETEK

My mother, Bronisława Markus, nicknamed Bronia or Bronka, grew up in Sandomierz, a picturesque town in southeast Poland on the cliffs overlooking the Vistula. It had been an important center for trade during the Middle Ages, and underground passages connecting the shops are still intact today. Although Sandomierz is mostly a Catholic city, its Jewish population, like Kraków's, has a long history. A synagogue built in 1768 still stands and is used to house government archives; the city experienced little physical damage during both world wars, but of course buildings do not tell even a part of the whole story of loss.

She was born in 1916, the middle child of three daughters, all of whom were legendary for their beauty. Her looks were truly remarkable—thick gorgeous hair, flawless complexion, a curvaceous figure and dark lashes and brows that enhanced the expressiveness of her blue eyes. Everyone took notice of her, yet she seemed unaware of how attractive she was and usually blushed when paid a compliment.

Her family came from great wealth and prominence. The Seijberts, her maternal grandparents, owned an expanse of land where they grew hops for Polish beer, and many Sandomierz residents worked for the Seijbert-Markus family, either in the fields or the family's brewery.

Bronia with her father, sisters, and cousins before the war

It was common in those days for scholarly men to marry into wealthy families like my grandmother's, so they could continue their studies without having to earn a living. And so it was that my mother was born to a wealthy heiress and a Talmudic scholar. Her father was an orthodox rabbi—intelligent and surprisingly open-minded. She recalled one incident when she had scarlet fever and was so ill that her parents were afraid she wouldn't survive. The family doctor examined her at their home and prescribed a rich diet of meat and cream. If it meant breaking kosher law to fight her fever, he advised, then break kosher. Without hesitation, my rabbi grandfather replied in his own language, "When it comes to someone's health, it is a sin *not* to break the rules."

Bronia grew up seeing her grandparents and sisters every day. Household servants tended to her every need, and she traveled to Paris with her personal seamstress to pick out fabric for her wardrobe. In her late teens she became a competitive ice skater.

But in September 1939, two weeks after German forces invaded Poland, the Nazis stormed my mother's hometown, and for two and a half years the townspeople awkwardly coexisted under the rule of their occupiers. When Sandomierz's feeble structure began to collapse in June 1942, the city's 2,500 Jews plus other Jews from the neighboring area were driven from their homes and herded into a ghetto community of some seven thousand people. Six months later, the Germans surrounded the entire Jewish area of Sandomierz and demanded that everyone vacate their properties, line up in the square, and prepare for immediate deportation. Both Jewish and non-Jewish citizens were shocked into submission, ill-prepared to oppose the Nazi invaders. The streets convulsed with people screaming, running, sobbing, and soldiers shooting. That night an eerie train whistle blew, as freight cars loaded with Jews rumbled away from Sandomierz. My mother's parents and grandparents were probably on that train.

Within a day or two, the Nazis had emptied the Sandomierz ghetto, shipping off a thousand citizens to a labor camp in Skarzysko-Kamienna. The rest were killed in the death camps of Treblinka and Belzec, where much of my mother's family must have perished.

My mother rarely spoke of her two sisters other than to mention that one was a gifted artist. She expressed sorrow and longing for them instead through the expression in her eyes. She never told us their names, but on the back of a photo of her older sister is the name "Rosia," who in the photo is young, fair haired, and beautiful. She, as I later learned, was the gifted sister, who worked for the Polish Resistance after the Nazi invasion. Since the photo is dated 1944, it is clear that Rosia made it almost to the end of the war before being captured and executed by the Germans.

My mother's older sister, Rosia, working for underground resistance, 1944

My grandparents tried to save my mother's younger, fifteen-year-old sister by giving money and jewels to a non-Jewish friend who promised to take her to a convent in England to wait out the conflict. The friend gladly accepted the money and valuables, but then turned the girl over to the Nazis, who slaughtered her. In this and similar ways, the Nazis picked off the Seijbert and Markus family one by one.

My father too was born into a family of wealth and prestige. Mieczyslaw Frydland, who everyone called Mietek, was born on February 8, 1911, and lived in a mansion on one of the most prominent streets in Warsaw with his sister, Genia, his younger brother, Josef, and his parents, Malka and Szymon. They also enjoyed a magnificent summer villa outside Warsaw, where they would host elaborate parties for family and friends, complete with exquisite dinners, a live orchestra, and dancing. The Frydland family manufactured felt for international clients who used it in pianos, furniture, ammunition, and other products.

My father was educated in private schools and university at a time when most Jews in Poland were not allowed an education beyond elementary school. As a young man, he traveled extensively and effortlessly throughout Europe, and because of his elite education and privileged lifestyle, developed an expansive knowledge of classical music, languages, poetry, and art. He was handsome and proud of his appearance, journeying all over Europe to find the perfect wardrobe: London to buy suits, Paris to buy shirts, and Rome to buy Borsalino hats. People were instinctively drawn to Mietek, a natural-born charmer, and he maintained long-lasting friendships and relationships with his peers and colleagues in the Warsaw business community. He was sensitive and caring, and treated family, friends, and servants generously. Eventually he married his first wife, Junia, and they had a little girl.

After his father died of cancer in the early 1930s, Mietek stepped in as chairman of the board for the family business, although he was considered by some to be too young to assume such an important position. Genia too worked for the company, but Josef, also well educated, preferred a playboy lifestyle—enjoying the privileges afforded him but never helping out.

My father, Mietek

By the early twentieth century, Warsaw had the largest Jewish population of any city in Europe. In September 1939, about a third of the city's population, more than 350,000, was Jewish—only New York City had more Jews. But in 1940, under the pretext of combating a typhus epidemic, the Nazis, using Jewish labor, began erecting walls around the ghetto. The walls were more than ten feet high, topped with barbed wire, and closely guarded.

On October 12, 1940, German Governor General Hans Frank issued the order to create the Warsaw Ghetto, and within a month had sealed it off from the rest of the city. Their project completed, the Germans forced 115,000 non-Jewish Poles to resettle outside the Jewish district, and corralled more than one hundred thousand Jews from other areas into the ghetto settlement. The ghetto population rapidly burgeoned to 450,000 people in an area of about 1.3 square miles. As the situation worsened, ghetto residents began collapsing from hunger and disease, or were transported to forced labor camps, where they perished. People lay dead in the streets.

Unable to imagine a situation in which their wealth and prestige would not save them, my father's family was about to learn a bitter truth. Like so many others, they underestimated the depth and breadth of the Nazis' hatred, much less their boundless capacity for savage cruelty. The Frydlands' wealth, rather than protecting them, made them glaring targets for brutality when the occupying Germans overtook Warsaw.

Their large, lavishly furnished home was an ideal spot for Nazi headquarters, since it was on the same street as the telegraph and communications buildings. The family business was likewise seized for military purposes, and all its assets were confiscated. Mietek, his wife and child, his mother, sister, in-laws, and servants were forced to leave their home and live together in the Warsaw Ghetto, and when the Nazis descended, randomly shooting on the ghetto one day in 1940, among those killed were most of the Frydlands, along with their servants.

My father and his brother-in-law had left the ghetto earlier that day to check their mail. It was an odd twist of fate that, on a day of no special significance, they left and made their way to the train station that served as a clearinghouse for information. The train stations were always jammed with people trying to get news—about loved ones, about the Allies' progress. Rushing back to the ghetto in time for the German-imposed curfew for Jews, Mietek and his brother-in-law encountered a man they knew, running toward them, sobbing. He told them of the attack on the ghetto, the murdering of women and children, executed in cold blood. Thunderstruck, they started toward the ghetto, but the man grabbed their arms to stop them. There was no reason to return, he warned them. They must try to save themselves. "If you die," he said, "the Nazis win."

My father lost his wife, his little girl, his mother, sister, and his entire way of life in one afternoon. He had no one and nothing left. He had nowhere to go.

*Bronia in Siberia with unknown people and
Polish uniformed soldiers, Photo by Mietek*

Chapter 3

THE UNSPEAKABLE COLD

By mere circumstance, my mother was away in Kraków while the Nazis were executing her family during their siege of Sandomierz. Bronia had married a man named Nathan, and with a toddler son in tow, they were attending medical school at the University of Kraków. Although Jews weren't normally allowed to enroll in medical school in Poland, good connections or enough money for a bribe could still secure placement.

As the Nazis gained power, they started rounding up Jews in Kraków, requiring them to have physical exams, and the doctor who examined my mother was one of her professors. Taking pity on her, and because she was blonde and blue-eyed, he listed her on the examination form as Irish-Catholic, an act that may have been a token of kindness, or perhaps it was a personal rebellion against Nazi prejudice. In either case he saved my mother's life, enabling her to escape with Nathan and their little boy to Ukraine and then Russia in an attempt to elude the Germans. They stopped running when they reached Siberia.

"One day I was being fitted for a new outfit by my seamstress," my mother recalled, "and the next day I was naked."

Between 1939 and 1941, nearly three hundred thousand Polish Jews—almost 10 percent of the Polish Jewish population—fled German-occupied Poland and crossed into the Soviet Union. Determined to get as far from the Nazis as possible, these Polish Jews sometimes walked for weeks and months. The more fortunate took slow, crowded, grime-coated trains that spewed black smoke along the Trans-Siberian Railway, connecting Moscow to the Russian Far East and the Sea of Japan. Whatever their means of travel, refugees in search of shelter haphazardly dispersed throughout Siberia and other Soviet-controlled regions. The Soviets, gearing up to fight their own war against the Germans, were rankled by this influx of desperate refugees.

Although Soviet authorities deported tens of thousands of Jews to Siberia and other remote areas, it appears my mother and Nathan went there on their own accord. Siberia was just one of a number of horrendous options available to them, and despite impossibly harsh conditions, those who escaped to USSR made up the largest group of European Jews to survive the Nazis.

The escape to Siberia was fraught with tragedy for Nathan and my mother. Their two-year-old boy starved to death on the arctic tundra. My sister Sarah was born in 1943 in a Siberian camp. After Sarah, my mother gave birth to another girl, who, for reasons she never fully explained, was taken from her by soldiers. The baby was never seen again. My mother refused to describe the circumstances that led to the kidnapping of this infant, and to this day the possible scenarios haunt me. As I mentioned earlier, my role in our family was to replace both my father's infant daughter and my mother's two children—my three half siblings. I was never told any of their names.

Soon after their son died, Nathan, for reasons unknown, deserted my pregnant mother and Sarah. He left without a word, and my mother didn't know where he went or if he was alive or dead. His disappearance was so sudden, she could only guess what might have happened to him, and since they were in hiding, she had to scavenge without his help for even the most meager of meals. In retrospect, she suspected he may have joined a military band, labor force, or some organized group as a way to eat, particularly since he had a heart condition that further weakened him.

She thought the starvation and cold had been too much for him to bear in hiding with his family.

Left alone with Sarah, my mother struggled to stay alive, eating frozen potato roots or anything she could find. Lactating women would feed as many babies as they could, so my mother determinedly nursed other children in the camp. She wrapped rags around Sarah's feet to keep her warm, and then used those same rags, when needed, to muffle Sarah's cries when Soviet soldiers were nearby. Interestingly, throughout her entire life, Sarah harbored a vague and haunting recollection of forced silence, fear, and darkness. Later, she became intrigued by the concept of compassion for the dying.

My mother never expressed any bitterness toward Nathan. In fact, she loved him so much that in later years she shrugged off his behavior, saying, "Men don't do well without food."

Sarah and unknown woman in Siberia

With no reason to stay in Warsaw, my father decided to head east, toward Russia, where he hoped he would be safe. "Safe" became a relative term, since his trek was extremely dangerous. German soldiers captured him on the journey, tied his hands behind his back, and rammed his neck onto a tree stump.

Dangling an axe over his head, they taunted him, pumping him for inside intelligence, and demanding that he turn over any money or gold he had.

Years later my father said, "I had some bills in a money belt, but I knew without this money to use for bribes, I was as good as dead anyway. So I refused to give them up." Unable to provide any information and unwilling to lose his money, Mietek awaited his beheading when, out of the blue, two SS officers arrived and began a heated debate with the soldiers interrogating my father. While they were arguing, Mietek saw an opportunity to escape and ran for his life, but he was later captured by the Russians, who imprisoned him. Records show his arrest in Belarus in 1940. With only a thin layer of clothing between their malnourished bodies and the icy arctic winds, prisoners in the prison camp were placed in quarters so packed and narrow they could barely move their limbs. They usually remained that way, pinned against a wall, until they were ordered out for interrogation and beatings. For the rest of his life, my father suffered the psychological effects of that prison camp; for example, he could never face the wall when seated in a restaurant. But the emotional repercussions were far more serious. He suffered from horrible nightmares, and became quickly agitated in close quarters, such as in a car. He would lose his temper for no apparent reason and go into pathological rages. He would also lapse into strange periods of silence and trembling, particularly when he was not in control of a situation. As a young man, he began to lose his hearing, a condition exacerbated by the torture he had endured. And later, partially due to his deafness, he had trouble sizing up a situation, either retreating inappropriately or demanding complete control and undue attention.

Eventually he was either released or escaped from that prison camp, and traveled to Siberia, where he met my mother. The family lore is that Bronia was walking in the cold, holding baby Sarah and carrying packages containing everything she owned. My father came to her rescue, offering to help her with the packages. She consented, and he stayed with her. They were still together when the Allied forces defeated the Nazis, freeing the prisoners and enabling Jewish refugees to exit Siberia.

My parents slowly made their way back to Poland, following the Russian front, to search for surviving family and friends.

When they finally reached Warsaw, they were heartbroken to see the unfathomable devastation around them and the extent of the Nazi massacre. By the time Soviet troops liberated Warsaw in January 1945, about 175,000 people—of the 1,000,000-plus prewar population—were left in the city, and only 11,500 of them were Jews. By the end of World War II, 98 percent of the Jewish population of Warsaw had perished, and only 50,000 Polish Jews chose to remain in the country. The atmosphere in war-torn Poland was rife with anger and anti-Semitism. Poland had turned its back on its own people, and most Jews were eager to get away.

When my mother returned to Sandomierz, only to find her family gone, everyone and everything she knew obliterated, she receded into a weary melancholy that enshrouded her for as long as she lived. She had fought countless battles on her children's behalf and still lost her son to starvation, her infant daughter stolen. After so many sorrows, so much resilience, she wrapped herself in a protective armor of dispassion. Bronia would later marry Mietek in Stuttgart in 1948—perhaps out of love, but more likely out of resignation. He had helped her and Sarah, so she felt she owed him. Even though she loved all her children, she was inclined to dismiss her surviving children's troubles, expecting us to be able to fend for ourselves, as she had. And so we did.

Children in DP camp, Berlin, 1947, Photo by Mietek

Chapter 4

"DA VORNE STEHT AMERIKA!"
("There Ahead Stands America!")

W hen the war ended, and it was clear that living in Poland was no longer an option, my parents entered Germany, moving from one displaced persons camp, or DP, to another, waiting for the opportunity to leave Europe. More than 250,000 Jews congregated in these camps, hoping they would be a brief stop on their way to a new life. But that wasn't always the case. Conditions were atrocious, only slightly better than in a Russian prison camp, and their stays were longer than they hoped for. A photo taken by my father shows a band of refugee children standing outside a cabin, some of the boys wearing little girls' ruffled blouses, which were probably the best clothes they could find.

Every day was a constant battle against lice, cold, and contagious diseases spread by dozens of people living shoulder to shoulder in single rooms. In 1945, President Harry S. Truman sent Earl G. Harrison as a representative of the Intergovernmental Committee on Refugees to inquire into the condition and needs of displaced persons in Germany. Harrison wrote in his report: "As matters now stand, we appear to be treating the

Jews as the Nazis treated them except that we do not exterminate them. They are in concentration camps in large numbers under our military guard instead of S.S. Troops. One is led to wonder whether the German people, seeing this, are not supposing that we are following or at least condoning Nazi policy."

My family was placed in Dueppel Center in the American Occupied Zone of Berlin, where 5,130 displaced persons—mostly families with children—were housed, and where, in the provisional hospital that served the camp, I was born. Eight to twelve people lived together in rancid, heatless rooms averaging twelve by fifteen feet. My mother spent many hours searching for places where food was being given to refugees, for enough food to feed the four of us. Coffee was a luxury, and my father, who had never tasted peanut butter, which the Red Cross offered as a protein supplement, thought it was some type of mortar and refused to eat it. He had good reason to be disgusted: during the war he had seen children trying to dull their hunger by chewing on chunks of mortar they found scattered throughout bombed-out buildings.

Refugee camps were sucking in and spitting out thousands upon thousands of homeless postwar wanderers every year. In fact, the last of the DP camps, Foehrenwald in Bavaria, remained in operation until 1957. Although their living conditions were heinous, there were some positive aspects for camp residents. Initially set up by the Allies, the camps were taken over by UNRRA, the United Nations Relief and Rehabilitation Administration—though the combined military forces continued to provide housing, security, and supplies, and voluntary organizations such as the Jewish Joint Distribution Committee and the Association for the Promotion of Skilled Trade (translated from Russian) established programs for survivors in Germany, setting up training centers in seventy-eight DP camps, helping nearly eighty-five thousand people acquire professions and skills to rebuild their lives.

After the Dueppel Center, we moved to a DP camp in Stuttgart. My parents were married in that camp on July 10, 1948, five months after I was born. The Dueppel Center in Berlin was evacuated in July 1948 as a result of the Berlin Blockade.

Later my family moved to DP Camp Mattenberg, Kassel-Ober-zwehren, about four hundred kilometers southwest of Berlin; then on July 21, 1949, south to Wildflecken (which housed as many as twenty thousand displaced persons); and then to the International Refugee Organization Emigration Camp in Butz-bach, north of Frankfurt.

One day, out of the blue, Nathan arrived at the Berlin DP camp in search of my mother. He tried frantically to persuade her to return to him with Sarah. My father became insanely jealous, but he took several photographs of Sarah and Nathan. Some were taken against a wall with weeds and flowers popping out of the concrete, and others at the beach. Someone took a photo of my father in a bathing suit, looking as though he is showing off his form. I can only guess at the kind of discussions that took place between Nathan and my mother. Clearly, she still loved him, but by now she had a child with another man. She must have felt torn, already having learned how difficult my father was.

In the end she made the decision to stay with Mietek, since he had helped her when she was alone and abandoned in Sibe-ria. But I cannot help wondering what my life might have been like if my mother had made a different decision and gone away with Nathan. Years later, when Sarah and I were adults and she had only just discovered that her real father was not Mietek, my mother confided that "When I turned Nathan down, I made the worst choice in my life."

My earliest memory of these camps is a German cradlesong. While my mother went to work painting flowers on porcelain china, she left my sister and me in the camp with a babysitter. I remember our sitter's beautiful singing voice and the gentle, lilting tune she sang to us that clearly defined it as a lullaby. I recall a few of the lyrics, the slow tempo, each syllable softly but clearly articulated, and years later I sang it to my brother and sister when they were babies.

Die Negre mama . . . Und der Negre Papa . . . la, la, la, la, la, la, und so gehen Sie zu kleines Baby zu schlafen, und nicht weinen, nur schlafen . . . schlafen gehen . . . la, la, la.

("The Negro mama . . . and the Negro papa . . . and so the little baby goes to sleep, and not crying, just sleeping, sleeping, and goes to sleep . . .")

I have always wondered why there would be a song about black parents in Germany. Was it a folk song? There must be a trail of lullabies sung by black nurses in America. Where did the singer learn it? Was it a song from her childhood?

Ruth and babysitter, Berlin, 1947

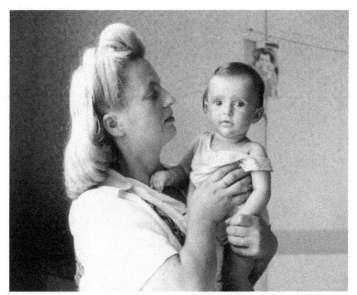

Bronia and Ruth, Berlin, 1947

I also have memories of my mother singing *Carmen* to me in Polish. Whenever I hear the melodies from that opera, I automatically insert the Polish words in my mind, even while it is being sung in Italian. I can still see my mother's blonde hair and feel the warmth and humor in her voice.

Eventually, my family made it to Camp Grohn in Bremen, which was the final stop for all displaced persons emigrating on ships from Bremerhaven. Like so many displaced Jewish refugees, my parents had waited almost four years for the proper sponsorship that would allow them to emigrate. My father had an uncle who had settled in California in 1928 and who would be a supporter for us. According to the Immigration Act of 1948, to emigrate to the United States, a displaced person needed a sponsor—someone who arranged for housing and employment, the latter which would not replace an American worker. Among the many documents I now possess are the countless applications and requests for visas, statements of birth and nationality, since their original papers had been lost. In 1949, the authorities finally gave my family the documents we needed to enter the United States.

UNITED STATES
DEPARTMENT OF JUSTICE

IMMIGRATION
AND
NATURALIZATION
SERVICE

*Alien Registration
Receipt Card*

Registration Number

7302380

FORM 1-151 (1-14-49)   16—48499-3

This is to certify that
    Ruth Friedland
was admitted to the United States on Sept. 4, 1949
at New York
as a N.P. Quota   immigrant for Perm. res.
under Sec. P.L. 774 of the Act of
and has been registered under the Alien Registration Act, 1940.
Visa Application No. 1   164829

DATE OF BIRTH	SEX	HAIR	EYES	HEIGHT
02-20-1947	F	Blond	Brown	3-4

Commissioner of Immigration and Naturalization.

GPO   16—48499-3

My immigration and naturalization cards, 1949

The days approaching our sailing were jubilant. My mother said she thought she was dreaming, going off to a new land where there would be plenty for everyone. Leaving war-torn Europe and the wretched camps was now becoming a reality. My parents packed all the years of paperwork, photographs, and passports into parcels, along with a few items of clothing and ribbons for Sarah's and my hair. My father took marvelous photographs of us as young émigrés, which he later framed and which proudly graced our table or mantel in our future homes.

We left Bremerhaven on August 25, 1949, on a seemingly endless sea voyage, sailing on the US Army transport ship *General M.B. Stewart*. I caught the measles and was quarantined in the ship infirmary, where I cried and cried—sick, scared, and alone. My mother would peer at me through a little window in the infirmary door, and I gagged in the fear that doctors would never allow me to be with her again. The only way the nurses could quiet me was to give me a banana, which was, after the unappealing food supplied by the Red Cross in the camps, a huge treat. Other than that, I was inconsolable.

Although he had been a seasoned traveler, Daddy couldn't handle the rough seas we encountered on this journey and felt seasick much of the time. On the other hand, when he wasn't leaning over deck to vomit, he was photographing the ocean scenery. His love for photography and his prewar ability to have the finest of everything included his having the best camera possible—and to him that was a Leica. Whether he purchased it on the black market, or found it another way, I'll never be sure. But on this journey, he captured a beautiful image of the ocean liner RMS *Queen Elizabeth* passing us as we sailed to America.

My father and mother were determined to forget, to rise above the past and shut out the atrocities they'd so recently endured. Unfortunately, what they'd experienced was too horrific to leave behind, and the future that awaited them in the land of liberty was far from certain.

By the time we pulled into New York Harbor on September 4, 1949, I was out of quarantine. As I stood on the deck, I spotted the Statue of Liberty and screamed at the top of my lungs, *"Da vorne steht Amerika!"* ("There ahead stands America!"), which made my parents proud. They repeated this story throughout their lives. My exhilaration upon seeing the Statue of Liberty stayed with me, and I was a very patriotic child. Sarah taught me the Pledge of Allegiance before I started school, and I spent hours alone, reciting it out loud, as if it were a mantra or some special prayer that would protect me from harm.

Arriving in New York was overwhelming for us. After all my family had been through, both during and after the war, we were finally free. I was two years old when we first stepped on American soil. After a brief stay in New York, we were transferred by the Jewish Welfare Service to Missouri, and provided a room in a run-down residential hotel in St. Louis where drunks regularly puked in the garbage-strewn staircases. Eager to leave this flophouse, we soon relocated to Los Angeles. My mother had dreamed about walking down the streets of America and picking oranges off the trees—and here we were, California bound, where such trees actually did bloom.

After so many travails, our family was on the verge of making a home in America—not just anywhere America, but Los Angeles, California. Land of orange trees and sunshine. Land of wealth, glamour, and movie stars. Land of Beverly Hills, Malibu Beach, and Hollywood. We would be living only six miles south of Hollywood!

We were heading to City Terrace, a shabby urban ghetto set aside for European war refugees. City Terrace is where the Jewish Welfare Service settled us, and where my family would hunker down and try to heal.

Chapter 5

CITY TERRACE

Ruth and Sarah in America

City Terrace may have been in a seedy area of East Los Angeles, but we were able to join similarly crippled refugee families there, and that made all the difference. People around us understood where we came from and what we had endured in our all-too-recent past. We developed close relationships with these families because everything about our new American life was foreign to us at the beginning. Everyone had language problems. The adults spoke little or no English, and even as they learned, they had strong accents and couldn't always make themselves understood. Often they would ask their Americanized children to make phone calls for them to avoid confusion.

No matter what their status had been previously, refugees soon discovered that they were at the bottom of the social pecking order in their adopted country. Although they had defied amazing odds to make it through the war, they were disdained and scorned by many, including, surprisingly, American Jews, even relatives, as we would soon learn.

During its heyday, City Terrace had been the "in" place for Jewish families. Unfortunately, we just happened to miss that era by about twenty-five years. City Terrace and the neighboring Boyle Heights were a mecca for Eastern European Jews in the 1920s and 30s. The Breed Street Shul in Boyle Heights—built in 1923 and now a historical landmark—was one of the oldest synagogues on the West Coast. As Jews poured into this area, the Boyle Heights Jewish population swelled from three families in 1908 to ten thousand people in 1930.

City Terrace was considered a more prosperous, more Orthodox neighbor of Boyle Heights back then. In addition to the predominantly Jewish residents, Japanese, Serbian, Italian, and Latino families filled the apartments. Yiddish was spoken on the streets, and signs were posted in Yiddish, Hebrew, and English.

By the time we arrived, however, most of the Jews had migrated to West LA and to the San Fernando Valley farther east. In their wake, they left the hardscrabble remains of a once glorious neighborhood—a parting gift to the new stream of impoverished refugee families like ours. It was into this community that the four of us—eight-year-old Sarah, my mother, my father, and I—were settled, in our first real apartment in the USA.

It was located around the corner from a small grocery store that had a big barrel of briny sour pickles just outside the door. My father would let us each pick one while he chatted with the owner, Heimie. The air in the store was ripe with cooking odors of familiar European foods—onions, cabbage rolls, and goulash, beef, rice, and barley soup. On the sidewalks we could hear whispering, bantering, and arguing in a polyglot of Yiddish, German, and Polish. City Terrace was like a neighborhood straight from a Hollywood set, an exaggerated representation of reality. In truth, however, it was a pulsating multiethnic community within a short range of the iconic Hollywood sign and completely devoid of glamour.

⁓

When we first moved there, my father's uncle, Sol, and his wife, Minnie, well established in the United States before the war began, were our sponsors. We thought this meant they would help us get settled, find jobs, and become respectable Americans. We had completely overestimated their willingness to become entangled with us, and were only invited to their lavish Beverly Hills home once or twice. As I mentioned before, Jewish refugees were often disdained by American Jews, even those to whom they were closely related.

Great-Uncle Sol had a son, William, and two grandchildren, Susan and David. Although we met only briefly, I remember them from the few encounters and from some stories I had been told. Why they were so elusive is a family mystery. I suppose they felt above us in social stature because they immigrated before WWII, totally out of harm's—and the Holocaust's—way. They seemed to have mastered the English language and were successful enough in business to live among the wealthiest people in Beverly Hills.

What stands out strongest in my mind is not their indifference to us but my mother saying, "William died in my arms." In the early 1950s, my mother worked as a practical nurse at Los Angeles County Hospital while going to nursing school to earn her credentials as a Licensed Vocational Nurse. William had been hospitalized for liver cancer when he was forty-two years old, and my mother, visiting him at the hospital, had her arms around him when he died. It must have been a crucial and emotional moment for her, because she repeated this whenever these family members were mentioned in our home. This was surely a tragedy for Uncle Sol and Aunt Minnie, but they never showed any warmth or compassion toward my mother or anyone in my family.

My first recollection of meeting my second cousins Susan and David was at their home, and the second one at our home when they came to visit for a family celebration. Susan was attractive and always well dressed. She was closer to Sarah's age, and either very shy or just quiet. David was my age, also not talkative, and kept close to his grandparents. Looking back, I don't think they ever considered us part of their family. We just came to accept this and go about our lives without expecting to have bonds with these relatives, which was a pity, since so few of our family members were alive after the war, and we would have cherished them. We had very few material possessions, and certainly the war had ravaged any semblance of success or youthfulness to my father's younger self, so Uncle Sol probably did not recognize this broken, tormented version of his nephew. Many years later, my father told me that David had died at forty-five during an emergency airlift to Philadelphia for a liver transplant, fighting the same illness that had killed his father, William.

Left to right: Bronia, my Uncle Josef's wife, Roselle,
Ruth, Sarah, and Tante Minnie in City Terrace

Uncle Sol and Aunt Minnie occasionally visited us, bringing shopping bags of what they called "old clothes" as gifts for our family. "Old clothes" was a generous term for what was in those bags. We would have loved and appreciated gently used hand-me-downs. Instead the bags were filled with moth-eaten sweaters, items that had been bleached beyond any color recognition, and socks with holes in them. We enthusiastically inspected the contents of these bags whenever they came and ultimately threw out everything. Privately, we referred to them as *Uncle Sol und Tante Minnie mit die shmattehs* (Uncle Sol and Aunt Minnie with the rags).

On the other hand, at least initially, we truly did live like vagrants. Our entire household furnishings consisted of one iron-framed bed, two pillows, a wooden kitchen table, and chairs. That was it—we didn't even have pillowcases. The mattress was so lumpy and threadbare that one night Sarah rolled over and caught her thigh in one of the iron springs. For the rest of her life, she carried a scar on her leg from that hazardous bed.

My mother got a job in a ketchup factory before going back to college, but my father couldn't find work. The factory job was a huge step down from being a medical student before the war, but given all the loss in the years since 1939, she was grateful for any job to earn money. Although she stayed pretty closed-mouthed about her situation, she was clearly disgusted by the way this factory operated. For several years, she refused to let us have any ketchup products in our house.

As for my father, he was understandably less fortunate in finding work when we first arrived in America. At some point as a young man, he had begun to lose his hearing. By the time I was a toddler, he was almost deaf, and I have no recollection of a time when he could hear. As a child, I just accepted that my father was deaf, but only recently learned that his hearing loss started before the war. Josef, in a letter written in Polish dated December 27, 1945, asked, "How about your ears? I've got the same problems as you and my hearing is seriously impaired. I don't know what to do, as there is no cure for this." Perhaps the deafness was a lifelong side effect of typhus. Or maybe deafness ran in the family.

In any case, his struggle to learn English was made all the more difficult because, initially, he couldn't afford a hearing aid. Unable to hear or comprehend all that was being said to him in an unfamiliar language, he became adept at reading lips—and after a while he purchased an old-style hearing aid that created a lot of background noise. I didn't consider until I was much older how isolating his handicap must have been for him. Deafness contributed to his inability to fit in—he spoke too loudly when engaged in routine discussions, he was immune to nuance and inflection in conversations, and he often responded inappropriately when people made innocent remarks. These reactions were not only due to deafness but also to his mental condition, which was fragile to begin with and which devolved as he was forced to adjust to his alien situation. The trauma of the war, the loss of loved ones, fleeing, torture, his arrest and internment in Russia that included more torture, then ending up in Siberia where he endured constant hunger and cold—all this left him in a mental state from which he could not recover. If he made new friends, they were almost always Europeans who spoke in the languages he knew best.

Being unemployable was emasculating for him. He had many talents and had always succeeded in business and in his hobby of photography. When he wasn't job hunting, he socialized with other refugees in our community, and saw to it that I was cared for while Sarah was at school. He walked me to the Hebrew Folk School for pre-kindergarten and picked me up at the end of the day.

Although our apartment was mostly bare, with only a few essentials provided by the owner and the Jewish Welfare Service, somehow my father saw to it that the hardwood floors were always waxed and polished to a shine. The living room was empty of furniture, but the floor was so smooth that Sarah and I would slide across it, wearing our socks and pretending we were skating. We may have been penniless, but we were clean, and the faint but pleasant odor of soap and bleach pervaded our apartment. After work, my mother would wash and starch her white nurse's uniform and cap (and the ribbons for our hair) to be ready for the next day. Except for the awful bed, I loved our first apartment in City Terrace.

Our next apartment was not far from the first one, but the rooms were bigger and we had more room to play outdoors. For the first time, I lived around non-refugee children and found myself jealous of the little girls with blonde hair in ponytails, dressed up and carrying tiny handbags. They looked so sophisticated, so American, so much like natural Californians. I was only allowed to wear dresses for birthday parties. The rest of the time I was clad in overalls or shorts and sunsuits, depending on the season.

The day my father showed up with a brand-new piano for our apartment was a tremendous surprise. There stood a walnut-cased upright piano and bench. We still didn't have pillowcases, but we had a beautiful new piano. The ivory keys appeared too smooth to touch. Sarah and I stood in awe—just staring at it, as if in a dream, afraid to get too close, as if that would somehow make it disappear. Finally, we pressed down the keys, listening to the melodious and dissonant sounds that came out. A wooden engraved plaque on the music rack read: *To Sarah and Ruth with love from Mother and Father.*

I could read pretty well by that time—Sarah taught me everything she learned in school when she came home—so I often stared at that engraved plaque. This piano, my parents were saying, represented love—a message that over the years I would find agonizing.

We were the only refugee children in our little community who had a piano, although I grew up thinking that the others had pianos and took lessons too. It wasn't until I was an adult that I learned otherwise. My mother spoke excitedly about music being the "universal language" and the one thing we could hang on to forever. "Nobody can ever take away your music and your education," she insisted. "People can take away your money, your clothes, your house, and everything else, but they cannot take away your music."

From the day it arrived, the piano became a source of joy and refuge in my life. The lady upstairs from our City Terrace apartment played the piano, and Sarah and I copied what we heard and played it by ear. The lady started giving Sarah piano lessons for twenty-five cents. My mother figured that for fifty cents a week, we both could have lessons. That's how my musical career began and continued throughout my childhood—playing a piano decorated with a plaque that memorialized our parents' love for us.

Sarah's influence on me throughout my life was profound. As a pre-schooler, I idolized her, as did every child in our refugee group. She had wavy brown hair, always involuntarily decorated with a bow, and dark brown eyes. When she was tired or upset, her eyes appeared to be brooding under her brow, but otherwise she had a beautiful smile for everyone. Although her usual disposition was outgoing and self-assured, she also had moody moments. The wartime and postwar experiences shadowed her, causing an illusory darkness she couldn't articulate. Still, as the oldest of this group of children, she had the self-confidence of a queen. She would line up all of us and order us around. And we would do anything for her—she was amazing, awe-inspiring, and a celebrity in our eyes.

She advanced quickly with her piano lessons, while, being four years younger, I trailed behind. We were different in our attitudes and approach: while she played swiftly and musically right from the start, she could never achieve the hand position and finger techniques that our teachers demanded and that I was able to accomplish. Sarah always spoke about how mean our teachers were, whereas I really liked them. I didn't mind practicing all the exercises and little pieces over and over again, and I never felt any competition between us. We were quite independent of each other with our lessons and practicing, yet some sibling rivalry must have existed with her, because whenever I got a new piece, Sarah would remark, "Finally!" It made me feel as though I was supposed to keep up with her.

In those early years, although I was introverted by nature, I was unburdened by inhibitions or self-consciousness, until it came time for auditions and competitions. Sitting on the bench outside a judge's office or backstage, I had so many butterflies in my stomach I could barely sit upright. But when I played, I felt pure joy. Performing just seemed to be instinctive to me.

My parents insisted on finding the best piano teacher for us, regardless of our family income, and they made lessons a top priority. I know they sometimes ran up debt, because they couldn't always afford to pay for so many lessons. But I was motivated by my mother's pride. She nurtured my love for the instrument, and I became a pianist because of her encouragement, insistence, and involvement. Surprisingly, many years later, I overheard my father telling someone about my musical experiences as a young child, recounting every detail of my playing, down to the scales, arpeggios, and other exercises, as well as the little pieces by composers Bach, Haydn, Mozart, Schumann, Kabalevsky, and Bartok that I had loved to practice. I was stunned by his recollection, because I had no idea he had been aware of my passion. He certainly never appeared to take notice at the time.

When Sarah and I were not practicing, my father would dust, polish, and buff every inch of the piano. It always looked new. The piano represented the riches he had lost from his privileged upbringing and would never be able to retrieve, like the lavish grand piano his family had had in their Warsaw home. He was so accustomed to the finer things in life, it seemed natural to take out a loan to purchase a new piano and have a customized plaque engraved. Most likely, my mother was not consulted about buying it. When it came to such decisions, my father allowed her no voice. Even as a destitute immigrant, he still envisioned himself as a wealthy aristocrat with a rightful place in high society.

Regardless of our family's postwar financial status, which ranged from lower to lower-middle class, my father always liked the finer things in life. He was a chimera of contradictions, making a point of dressing well, even when he was working in a meatpacking factory. He loved to listen to music even though he was essentially deaf, and he collected recordings by Edith Piaf, Maria Callas, Enrico Caruso, performers of Beethoven, and Eastern European cantors. Somehow he knew the music so well that he was able to enjoy it, possibly through the vibrations. In social settings, he was often the most charming person in the room, yet he could transform into an uncontrollable tyrant at home. We all breathed a sigh of relief when he went out for a walk or to visit other refugees.

Although he smiled and told jokes, my father was irreparably damaged by his war experiences. Until his death, he was consumed by the irretrievable prewar past, oblivious to the present and the need to adapt to it. He pined for the years when he enjoyed wealth and would sometimes shout, "I am the Prince of Poland!" In truth, he was not the Prince of Poland. He was, sadly, one more peculiar and penniless misfit living in City Terrace, California.

Sam Jackson, Esther Jackson, Cesia Kingston,
Bronia, Morrie Kingston, Photo by Mietek

Chapter 6

OUR CROWD

The strong bonds we made with other recently settled Jewish refugees in City Terrace offset our disappointment over Uncle Sol and Aunt Minnie's rejection. We became particularly close with two of these families, the Jacksons and the Kingstons. We all served as each other's surrogates for relatives who did not survive the war. I was a double surrogate—for my mother's and father's dead children and for dead relatives belonging to our new friends.

Struggling to gain a foothold, these families brought European culture and traditions to America, joining up for long walks after dinner, relaxing in gardens together to rehash the day's events. We lived in a neighborhood like no other, cemented by inextricable relationships borne of all the losses its residents had endured. Stripped of family, assets, and possessions, individuals formed new families, nonbiological replacements for past loved ones. Much would remain unspoken in this group. Tied together by the common threads of horror, survival, and gratitude, we understood each other well. Even now, although geography divides us, we still find ways to reunite for special occasions, celebrating birthdays, anniversaries, weddings, and seders. When children of the survivors married, they always included members from their former City Terrace support group on their guest lists.

❧

Like my parents, Esther and Sam Jackson were originally from Poland. Their daughter, Bella, became my lifelong friend, and was, like me, born in Germany. Her parents had returned to Poland after the liberation, but then traveled to Germany to scan bulletin boards in search of surviving family and friends. Esther gave birth prematurely to twin girls at Mannheim General Hospital, but tragically, Bella's twin sister died only two or three days after birth. Because of the twins' premature birth, Esther was unable to breastfeed for very long. Sam's sister, Frieda, whose daughter, Eda, was born just a few days after Bella, came to the rescue and was Bella's wet nurse. Both Esther and Sam had survived the Nazi concentration camps. I once asked Sam why he had numbers tattooed on his arm. With tears welling in his eyes, he silenced me. "This is something you shouldn't know."

Initially sent to Auschwitz, Esther was then transferred to a work camp in Poland to make backpacks for the *Wehrmacht* (German unified armed forces). She stayed there until the Russians liberated Poland. When the family came to America, they changed their name from Jachamovicz to Jackson. Their New York relative had changed his name to Jackson, so Sam did the same, and now he had a new American name. Esther and Sam were willing to do any kind of work to make a living. Although she knew no English, Esther got a job in a cafeteria and also took in sewing, while Sam worked as a tailor, and they eventually were able to go into business for themselves. They bought and sold a variety of businesses, including a drugless drugstore, a partnership with the Kingstons, a liquor store in Hollywood, and a delicatessen known for mile-high sandwiches and amazing potato salad. They toiled with one goal in mind: to create an easy life for their daughter. Esther might have been up to her elbows in potato salad, but she was content as long as Bella was well cared for.

Bella and I had similar coloring and began to look even more alike as my father took us to his barber for our identical haircuts—short bobs with bangs often pulled to the side with a large satin ribbon. This must have been a traditional European style, because we certainly didn't look like typical California girls. Heimie at the neighborhood grocery store would say to me, "Hi, Bella, it's nice to see you." And I would reply, "I'm not Bella, I'm Ruthie." We were often mistaken for each other, because we really did look quite similar back then.

As much as we may have looked alike, our family lives couldn't have been more different. I was envious of how Bella's parents doted on her, and I coveted her clothes closet with its rows of lovely dresses and skirts. Bella's bedroom was decorated with beautiful pink and blue ballerina wallpaper, and blonde wood furniture that could have come straight out of *I Love Lucy*. My family couldn't afford to worry about décor. I was grateful just to have a bed to sleep in with springs that didn't bite into my flesh.

Although the Jacksons were able to rise above their immigrant status and purchase all kinds of luxury goods, my father, still mired in prewar social hierarchy, felt superior to Bella's family. Clinging to the aristocratic line he had come from even as the world evolved around him, he ignored the fact the Jacksons now had more money and better housing than he did. Life, he believed, was cruel and unfair, and in his best "Prince of Poland" posturing, he reminded us that the Jacksons were uneducated and lower class compared to him.

⁓

My first memories of Morrie and Cesia Kingston, whose name (a translation of Kings-Stone) had been changed by Morrie's great-uncle Shea when they came to America, was when they both worked for Karl's Shoe Stores. The store sold relatively cheap shoes for the masses, and Morrie supplied shoes not only for the Jewish refugee kids, but also for the children in the neighborhood. Soon the Kingstons jumped into the world of American commerce and started buying various businesses, including a laundry plant and a knitting mill, where they both worked. Having survived being Jewish around the Nazis, they had become fearless. A new business venture never scared them. And Morrie, who had fled Poland with his mother during the war, was a superb businessman with a keen eye and wonderful sense of humor.

When Cesia first came to America, she was surprised that no one wanted to hear about her experiences during the war. People would say, "You're in America now, don't worry about it." The Americans made her feel as if her experience in Auschwitz had been no worse than a bad shopping day. Even the American Jews didn't want to know. Perhaps it was too soon and too raw. Perhaps people wanted to avoid unpleasant reminders of their own vulnerability. Perhaps no one wanted to feel threatened or face the pervasive guilt vibrating like white noise in the background of their minds. American Jews seemed embarrassed by the new Jews from Europe; maybe they actually believed some of the "dirty Jew" propaganda that had poisoned Europe. So Cesia kept mostly quiet about her war experiences, though to her daughter Marylin she described the cow she saw one day grazing in the field at Auschwitz, and how she had dreamed beyond the barbed wire, wishing she could be that cow, so fat and happy. Cesia understood the irony of feeling so debased that she'd prefer to be an animal rather than be treated worse than an animal in the concentration camp. But she temporarily closed that chapter of her life while she threw herself into her new American world, often remarking, "I never imagined that my life would be this great."

Many years later, with a change in public attitude toward the Holocaust, Cesia became active in survivor organizations and spoke extensively about her experiences during the war. She was an especially gifted speaker and attracted large audiences from all over the country. Like so many other survivors, she realized the importance of giving testimony to the atrocities she had endured and witnessed. Cesia was among the first survivors selected to be interviewed for Steven Spielberg's Shoah Foundation project. Here is a portion of what she wrote about her life after Germany invaded Poland in 1939:

> *My parents tried to maintain some semblance of normal family life. Our family pooled our food so that one child would eat just enough not to be hungry that day. This plan quickly failed. With each new increase in work quotas came a decrease in food rations and there was not*

enough food to make this plan work. I spent much time longing for a potato peel. My baby sister was born in the ghetto. I spent hours describing to her how a flower looked and how an egg tasted. I also promised her that one day she would taste chocolate. I think she believed me. She was killed in Auschwitz at the age of three, never knowing what it was like not to be hungry.

In August of 1944, our misery intensified. We were herded into cattle cars destined for Auschwitz—one of the last transports out of the ghetto. At the point of Dr. Mengele's baton, my mother and baby sister were pushed to the left, my older sister Nadzia and I were pushed to the right. Amidst unfathomable chaos, my mother told us, "You two can survive if you stay together. I am going to stay with the baby."

It was the last time I saw my mother and baby sister. My parents, one brother and one sister were killed in Auschwitz. Nadzia and I somehow survived the incomprehensible pain of Auschwitz, and were sent to another concentration camp named Stutthof. In January 1945, after three degrading, dehumanizing months there, we were forced on a death march to the Baltic Sea. All around us, women were dying from starvation and the cold since we walked barefoot in the snow with little clothing. Those who could not keep up were shot. When we reached the sea the Nazis were pushing everyone onto boats that were riddled with holes, intending to drown us all. Somehow, at the moment we were being forced onto the boat, the Allied forces flew overhead. We ran to hide. My sister and I spent the remainder of the war in a series of labor camps posing as Catholic girls.

The Jacksons, Kingstons, and Frydlands (soon to be Friedlands) were all enamored of our new American freedom and beautiful California.

Once we became naturalized citizens, we, like many immigrants, changed the spelling of our names to be more Americanized. Sometimes they missed; my mother wanted to be called Bernice, since it sounded so American, but the spelling change went from Bronizlava to Broniz. No one ever pronounced it correctly, but it did not seem to bother her.

Sometimes we would all pile into a car and go to a park for a picnic. Once, when everyone was new to LA, we stopped at a lovely green area and spread our blankets. The moms unpacked the food as the kids ran off and began to play. Suddenly, a grumpy man came hurtling out of his house and confronted us.

"What in the hell are you people doing here?" he demanded.

Offended, Sam and Morrie replied, "We are in a park having a picnic with our kids."

"You're not in a park!" the man sputtered. "You're on my front lawn! You got five minutes to pack up and get out of here or I'm calling the police."

Embarrassed, Sam and Morrie shouted to their entourage, "Pick up your things, kids, we are ruining this nice gentleman's beautiful lawn." So the three families quietly gathered up the food and children, and made a quick getaway.

Most of my happy childhood memories, it seems, happened away from my house, like the times Morrie and Cesia picked me up on their way to Lake Arrowhead or Big Bear. Sarah, being older, was active in school clubs and had more freedom, managing to stay away from home as much as possible. But for me those trips were as close to nirvana as I thought I would ever get. We'd go swimming, to restaurants, out for ice cream, and it was perfect—a change from my own family's activities. At night I'd sometimes get scared and crawl into bed with Morrie and Cesia, but they never said a word. They didn't know what was going on in my house, or about the tension that I felt in my own home.

In our community, we were known as "greeners," a derogatory term derived from "greenhorns," long used to describe all kinds of refugee immigrants from Europe. Being called greeners didn't faze us much. Our crowd had been called much worse, and we teased each other about being so new and clueless. For years, the adults would joke about a time when one of the women, who like most was out hustling to find a job, saw a sign: "Bookkeeper Wanted." She turned to her friends and said, "I'm going to apply for this job. I can hold a book!" On another occasion, Esther proclaimed, "I really want a sundae." Surprised, Cesia turned to her and said, "So order it." Esther responded, "You can only order it on Sunday." Cesia explained sundae, and they all laughed about it then and for the following fifty years. They could still make fun of themselves, laughing at their many faux pas.

A Bubba for Us All

Love permeated this group of immigrants. We all meant the world to each other, and to this day, the children of the survivors still refer to each other as relatives. Like soldiers in a small platoon, we completely depended on each other and shared anything we could, whether it was meals, money, childcare, or books. We even shared a grandmother. She was actually Morrie Kingston's mother, but she took on the role of *Bubba* (Yiddish for grandmother) to all the children. In our community, almost no one had extended family members still alive, so Bubba was a novelty in our neighborhood, and left a lasting impression on the children who knew her.

Bubba, I later learned, grew up in Kielce, Poland, and became a wife at age sixteen in an arranged marriage. She ran a vegetable cart in an open-air farmers' market in Lodz, and during a twenty-two-year period gave birth to ten children. Widowed in 1928, she was left with eight children after two had died. Whenever my parents mentioned Bubba, they always said in the same whispered breath, ". . . and she has only one kidney." This sounded exotic to me. I couldn't tell if it was a good thing or a bad thing, but it certainly made a person famous.

Bubba left Poland with Morrie and Cesia after the war. Morrie had saved money for their passage to the USA, and hid it in a locked suitcase under his bed. Like most women of her era, his mother believed in omens, and that through *tzedakah* (צדקה), or acts of charity, she could keep her family safe. So she cut a hole in Morrie's suitcase and handed out money to any survivor who needed it. She was not concerned about her own passage. Neither was Morrie. He believed that money paved the streets of America and he'd have no problem recovering all that his mother surreptitiously gave away. When they arrived in the United States, their entire net worth was five dollars.

Upon arrival, Morrie and Cesia had immigration papers, but Bubba did not. Somehow, she sweet-talked her way in by ceaselessly talking to and kissing the immigration person processing them. (Incidentally, Bubba's grandson, Abbe, now an immigration lawyer, says he has never had a client who talked and kissed her way into America.)

The Bubba I knew in City Terrace was old and wrinkled, and claimed she was too old to learn English. She usually wore a long skirt, men's tennis shoes, and a babushka, with her waist-length hair pulled tight into a bun. Even in her eighties, she was a force of nature, exuding remarkable energy and able to walk for miles. It wasn't unusual to see her trudging from the market with an enormous bag of potatoes. She cooked lamb chops for our lunches, baked challah every Friday, and made a daily pilgrimage to the bakery so her grandson would have a fresh cookie—a feat that turned out to be dangerous for all involved. Bubba didn't believe in stoplights or traffic signals. The local rabbi said he always knew when she was on her way because he'd hear brakes screeching and drivers shouting as she resolutely marched toward her destination.

Bubba babysat ten or twelve of us at a time. Our parents were either working or doggedly seeking employment, and she made sure all the children were safely walked home from school. On Sundays, she cooked large quantities of ground beef so all the survivor families could come to dinner. One of my favorite memories is of Bubba at my wedding. She was, as ever, nicely dressed in a babushka and comfortable shoes, and in the middle of the ceremony called out to me in Yiddish, "Turn around, Ruthelein! I don't believe it's you."

Abbe's bar mitzvah speech was all about Bubba. "Someone asked me if I knew how to make a bed. I replied, 'Yes, I do. You call Bubba.'" Years later, her granddaughter, Marylin, dedicated her doctoral dissertation to her, adding, "Of course Bubba would have surely said, 'Enough already!'"

Bubba was the original child advocate. Whenever anyone criticized a child, her common refrain was "Leave the kid alone." She died at age ninety-four, and her gravestone reads, ABOVE ALL SHE VALUED CHILDREN. But that is not her only legacy. She allowed me to imagine how it would feel to have a bubba of my own, and for her biological grandchildren, she still emanates a magical presence: a shelf in her granddaughter's dining room displays Bubba's chipped tin cup, the family treasure that it is.

The Jacksons' hard work paid off. They had saved enough money to leave our neighborhood and move up to West Los Angeles. After they left, I was lonely, even when my mother had a rare day off from work. We moved again within the same neighborhood in City Terrace—this time not to an apartment but to a real house with a massive front lawn, landscaped with flower beds and giant avocado, fig, and peach trees. It was adjacent to a church, and my father was hired to be the caretaker of the property, probably in exchange for some or all of the rent. The Jackson and Kingston families were frequent visitors from their West Side homes, but it still wasn't the same.

Our family walks through the neighborhood were now considerably longer, since we still didn't own a car and there was virtually no street life. We had lost something precious, but our lives moved on. Although we were no longer able to walk to the grocer, Sarah and I began walking to school, to the nearby beauty shop with my mother, and to the Terrace Movie Theater, which became an important social outlet. Sarah would take the younger refugee kids to the movies when their parents were visiting my family, certifying her position as an idol among us. Although she was only a few years older, Sarah was so innately self-possessed and confident that the grown-ups entrusted her to chaperone the rest of us. We, in turn, trailed after her like a phalanx of apostles, honored to have her lead us through the neighborhood.

Birthday party in City Terrace, Photo by Mietek

The children of the survivors in City Terrace seemed to fall into two groups. Some were overachievers because they believed it was expected of them and didn't want to disappoint their parents. In some respects, my family fell into this category. Sarah and I always tried to be perfect students, at school and at the piano.

The second group was so overprotected the children found it difficult to become autonomous. Their parents taught them to mistrust individuals outside the family. As a result, studies show a higher frequency of separation anxiety and guilt in children of survivors than in their peers. I had a neighborhood friend in the second group. An only child, her parents, both Holocaust survivors, carried her wherever she needed to go. They treated her like a fragile orchid, even though she was perfectly capable of walking. If there was the slightest wind, her parents wouldn't consider taking her outside. If someone coughed in an auditorium or theater, they quickly squired her away in their arms.

As she grew older, she started to defy her parents in every possible way. She began her rebellion by shoplifting, and later became a heroin addict. In protecting their daughter from every conceivable outside evil, her parents failed to protect her from herself. After years of self-destruction, my friend finally turned her life around in adulthood.

At times I was thrown into this second group. Because I was the firstborn postwar child, my father felt the need to control every aspect of my life, particularly as I became school aged. He did not even permit me to walk home from school by myself. By this time he had purchased a secondhand car, and as I exited the school building, I would see his dreaded green Pontiac idling in the parking lot, waiting for me, and my stomach knotted up.

Sarah was more fortunate. Because she was older and was going to junior high, she rode the bus to and from school, and after getting off at the bus stop, walked home with her friends. She often went to their homes after school to study or socialize, and one of her friend's parents would drive her home at night.

For the most part, our family didn't fit neatly into any mold. To our peers, we were just another kindred refugee family forging out a new existence. Sometimes our friends might have heard the yelling and the banging and the muffled sounds of children crying. They might have seen the bruises covering Sarah's and my arms and legs. They might have caught the pounding of chords or the *plink, plink, plink* of tiny, anxious hands tapping out tunes on the piano. But nobody else knew what daily life was like in the Friedland house.

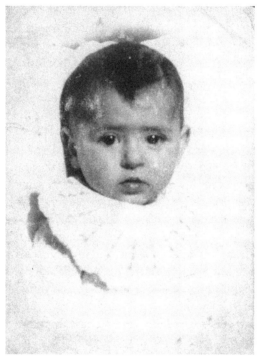

Mietek's first baby girl, Warsaw, 1939, Photo by Mietek

Chapter 7

REPLACING THE DEAD

I know so little about what my parents went through during the war, because they were reluctant to speak about it. I heard phrases such as "cattle cars," "we were in the Ukraine," "hunger," "unsanitary conditions," "lice," "facing death," "Nazis," "Communism," to name a few, but these were just amorphous words, their meanings too complex for me to appreciate. What they did tell me was too much too soon, and then they didn't want to talk about it anymore. As time went on, it became clear that they wished to forget whole chapters in their lives. World War II and its consequences became the elephant in the room. Our family just tiptoed around it and hoped it would go away. Needless to say, it did not.

Screams and nightmares were commonplace in our household, routinely jolting us awake in the middle of the night, only in our family it was my mother and father shrieking in terror, waking us as we cowered under the covers. I wanted to know the source of these screams, and yet I didn't want to know.

I learned not to ask.

⁓

When I was about five, I began to look through a box of photographs my father usually kept in their bedroom. In the box were originals and duplicates of the pictures he had taken of us or while visiting family friends. Many had dates, places, and notes about the events written on the back. In retrospect it's apparent that he had a sensitive eye for bringing meaning to what otherwise would seem routine and uneventful. He would spend an unbearable amount of time carefully composing each family photo with his Leica, and we'd plead with him, "Please, Daddy, hurry! Please, just take the photo." The many photos I still have look like typical family photos but with more thoughtful composition. Usually everyone in the photos is smiling and appears happy, but my mother's weary eyes, captured so poignantly by my father, betray her personal tragedies.

Although his behavior in seeking perfection while taking photos was close to maniacal, he was still a different person then, different than the father who went into screaming rages and bullied his wife and children. While the pictures reveal his attempt to portray a blissful life in America, I suspect he wanted to recreate the happier days of his life as well have physical proof that he was a good man with a nice family.

In a separate box hidden behind the other box were some shocking photographs that depicted life in the concentration camps—horrific images of starving, naked bodies, stacked one on top of each other in gruesome defeat. These images still haunt me today. A few years later, I revisited this box, which was no longer hidden but still separated from the family photos. The fact I had already seen them made them no less horrifying to view again. In fact, it was worse the second time because I understood clearly how these bodies came to be so, with hollowed-out eyes, sunken faces, barely any remaining flesh, approaching death or already dead.

*Mietek's mother, Malka,
and sister, Genia*

Genia and Josef, c. 1932

*Mietek's sister Genia, Warsaw 1938,
Photo by Mietek*

*Genia, previously a model for
Christian Dior, Photo by Mietek*

Malka portrait, age 16, Poland

Some of our family photographs had been sent to my father's uncle in the United States before the war, and given back to us when we arrived in California. These were kept in envelopes, apart from current ones, some marked by dates or locations. Through the years, my father continued to fill the photo box with new images of our family and friends in Los Angeles.

I thought I had seen all the photos, but years later, in the top dresser drawer in my parents' bedroom, I came across a picture of a baby with big dark eyes and a fancy lace collar. I used to like looking in that drawer, where I could smell the mahogany wood and see the green felt lining that protected their most sacred possessions. My mother kept the jewelry she never wore in there, and my father's watches were lined up neatly in place. At first I thought the baby in the picture was me, but as I studied it, I realized that this baby looked a little different. When I asked my mother about the photograph, she told me it was a picture of my father's daughter with his first wife, and that the little girl had been murdered by the Germans. For the first time, I began to learn about my father's previous life.

I still don't know this innocent little girl's name, but my heart aches to think about her and all the other children who never made it beyond their toddler years. Although I was only a young girl myself when I learned about the Warsaw Ghetto, seeing this picture made it a real place for me. I began to realize how my parents were haunted by the ghosts of beloved family members, including this baby, who had been senselessly killed.

When I was about four or five, my mother gave birth to my brother Simon, named after my father's father, Szymon. These were the days when children weren't allowed to visit in a hospital, so my father brought Sarah and me to a street near the hospital. We looked up to a window where my mother was waving and proudly holding up our new baby brother. Four days later, little Simon died, and something died inside my mother at the same time. She had lost her baby, and his death brought back all the other losses she had previously endured. Having yearned for a healthy American son, my mother was inconsolable.

When she got home from the hospital, she went to bed and stayed there. My usually active and beautifully put-together mother was like a zombie. She didn't speak, she didn't eat. When she did get out of bed, she wore a silky, dark-green, polka dot robe—her long blonde hair falling loose and disheveled. Her grief was palpable. A daughter had been snatched away and her firstborn son had starved to death in Siberia. How much tragedy could she bear?

The Jewish Welfare Service sent someone to take care of Sarah and me while my mother grieved. The lady brought with her a single doll and a few books about Moses. Sarah and I argued over the doll as it was the only one we had. We could tell something was wrong with our mom, but it didn't keep us from indulging in normal childish self-absorption. My mother eventually emerged from her catatonia, but Simon's death trailed her like a phantom for the rest of her life.

I can't remember the first time my father hit me; I feared him from an early age. He would often scream at my mother and push her around, but with Sarah and me he was far more physical.

We endured regular, almost daily beatings. Sometimes I wound up with welts on my body, but this was before the days of child protective services, so no one seemed to care that I had bruises and bumps. As I look back, his behavior was beyond erratic to the point of deranged. I never knew which Daddy was standing in the room.

His shouting at my mother was frightening, because I knew he would try to smack her and she would fight back. Then inevitably, one of them would leave the house. If Daddy left the house, he would return as though nothing had occurred, laughing and making jokes I didn't find funny or could not understand, bursting into laughter at his own humor. When my mother left the house, it was usually to go to work, so I wasn't able to see her until the next day.

Once I saw him pick up a hot iron and go toward my mother. I ran into another room, but I could hear the screams. I don't think he ever did more than threaten her with the iron, but he did chase her. I could not watch. As on many occasions when I was scared, I ran and hid under the bed.

When his anger was directed at Sarah or me, it invariably took us by surprise. We tried hard to avoid triggering his temper, and I never knew what I'd done to provoke him. I can still hear the sound of his belt swiftly unbuckling, and the horrifying swooshing sound as he slipped it from the belt loops of his pants. With mouth hardened and face tightened, he'd begin thrashing me and swearing in Polish, and I would fall to the floor—or if we were in the bedroom, I'd fall onto the bed while he continued flailing me. His was not a systematic spanking like many children grew up with. My father's method was haywire—indiscriminate abuse for some indecipherable reason. He did manage a few times to explain why I was being punished: he was looking for something and could not find it, or I had refused to eat my dinner, or Sarah or I did not hold our fork or knife properly.

Sarah was double-jointed in her fingers, so following his instructions for using utensils was difficult, and he would scream and slap her across her hands, then turn his screaming at me. Inevitably, one or both of us got clobbered. I usually went to sleep crying, in physical and mental pain, when my mother was at work. When she was home, she stayed away, probably knowing her interference would make matters worse. The slightest irritant would infuriate him. I guess he wanted us to grow up to appear as aristocratic as he was.

When I was six years old, my mother signed me up for a dance class at the Jewish Community Center. I was thrilled, although I often had welts and bruises on my legs, and was too embarrassed to go. I didn't want someone to notice, and I was sure the other little girls would make fun of me.

One Sunday morning, just before I was to go to my dance class, my father, for no obvious reason, went into one of his rages. As usual, I was stunned when he began beating me with his belt, and when he finally stopped, I fell to the floor in my dance clothes. "Mommy," I wailed after he'd left me on the floor in a fetal position, "why is Daddy doing this?" My mother shrugged and gave me her standard response to seeing her children slapped and punched until they were black and blue. "He's crazy," she'd sigh, and walk into the kitchen to fix dinner.

Needless to say, I was less outgoing than most kids, and the few friends I had were mostly from our City Terrace network. At school I knew other students, but for obvious reasons would never think of having them over to my house. I had few opportunities to do things after school, because my father made me come straight home. One summer Saturday or Sunday when I was about twelve or thirteen, I went to a nearby bowling alley with a girl from junior high. We were walking down Garfield Boulevard, and I remember feeling happy to be out of the house, looking forward to playing with my friend. Unfortunately, a Polish couple who were friends of my parents, Mr. and Mrs. Kwapish, drove past us and reported to my father that I had been walking the streets in shorts!

As soon as I came in the front door, my father flew into a rage, forbidding me to see the friend again, screaming and cursing and smacking me across the face. My mother stood by, a look of futility clouding her eyes. She did not come to my rescue by explaining to him that most girls in America wear shorts in the summer and that I should be allowed to walk with my friend dressed like that. Instead she kept silent and allowed my father to abuse and punish me for what we both knew was an innocent choice.

Throughout my childhood, those words "He's crazy" became the official explanation for my father's over-the-top tantrums. My mother proclaimed it so often that I grew up believing him to be certifiably insane. In fact, at least three times during my childhood, after some of his more explosive episodes, he was carted off to psychiatric hospitals.

As I got older and went to other families' homes, I started to realize that our family was not normal, and other fathers were not losing control of their tempers and beating their children. But for many years I had no idea how bizarre our family life was. If our teachers or neighbors noticed the ugly bruises erupting over our bodies, they never mentioned it or tried to intervene.

The day our neighbors Morrie and Cesia had their second child, Marylin, my father came to pick me up at the Jewish pre-school and we went directly to a toy store. The Kingstons weren't trying to be different or fancy in naming their daughter Marylin. They simply misspelled Marilyn. Often the last child to get picked up, I had been waiting, looking out and gripping the chain-link fence with my nose sticking through, like a tiny prisoner of war. But my excitement bubbled up when I realized where we were going.

A new baby for our close friends was thrilling, and when we got to the store, my father told the clerk he wanted the best toy in the store for a young boy.

"Why are you buying a boy's toy for a baby girl?" I asked.

"Oh, this gift isn't for the baby. It's for Abbe [the Kingston's older child]. I want him to really like me."

As an afterthought, my father bought the new baby a gift also, but it was clear to me, even then, that my father yearned for a son, especially after the tragedy of losing Simon.

I still remember Abbe's room, decorated to the hilt in a cowboy motif, where even the linoleum had cowboys on it. Abbe still remembers my father bringing him the gift—the only adult who thought to buy him something when Marylin was born.

It's now clear that my father was a muddle of conflicting, mixed-up emotions. At times he could be the world's most thoughtful, kind, and considerate person, showing warmth to

*Bella with two neighborhood children. Cowboy motif linoleum in
Abbe's room, Los Angeles, Photo by Mietek*

his fellow refugees, neighbors, friends, and relatives. His flip side
was brutal. The loss of his family, his wealth, and his comfortable life in Warsaw turned him into an unpredictable hydra. On
many occasions I would see him sitting at the kitchen or dining
room table with his head down, not sobbing, but unable to look
up because of his sadness or depression, completely despondent
and defeated. I didn't have to tiptoe around him anymore by the
time he lost his hearing, but I would watch him for long periods. At other moments I would find him sitting with a pencil,
sketching human figures in a room and around the borders of
that room, all drawn in perfect perspective. I wondered who they
were, if they were just imaginary figures or impressions of people
he once knew. Sometimes he would walk around the house without his hearing aid, ranting and raving, wearing only his boxer
shorts, his hairy chest and back exposed to the elements. A few
hours later, he would suddenly appear, dressed impeccably, looking dapper in a suit and tie, ready to visit friends.

My father's serious mental health issues made it difficult for
him to hold a job. He couldn't compete financially with his busi-
ness-savvy friends, and we kept moving from one questionable
location to the next as my parents tried to live in the cheapest

places in the best school districts they could afford. The piano with the plaque remained one of the few constants in our household.

Cesia Kingston and Esther Jackson were my mother's only friends during this period. At times they seemed to understand that "things were not good" at the Friedland home, or that our family was "having problems," but they never could have guessed the extent of the pathology—and no one ever told them. Yet they always showed up, when needed, to pick up Sarah or me and take us away from our father.

It's my belief that my parents became so twisted and damaged by their wartime trauma that, once free, they either administered or tolerated the same abuse they'd fought so hard to escape. (This was long before post-traumatic stress disorder might have been diagnosed.) Survivors were left to build new lives and fend for themselves without much medical care. Mental health care in the 1950s was primitive by today's standards. Few medications were available, and it was generally considered a sign of weakness to seek help for mental problems.

Bronia and Mietek in Siberia

Eventually, Daddy was able to land a job at a meatpacking plant, working at a physically demanding job on the midnight shift. He had initially been given a better time slot, but his boss transferred him to the graveyard shift when he proved unable to get along with his coworkers. It was an insult for the "Prince of Poland" to be reduced to such debased manual labor, but our family needed the money. Otherwise we'd never be more than a cluster of immigrants stuck forever in City Terrace housing, accepting handouts from the ladies of the Jewish Welfare Service.

Mietek 1947, Berlin

Malka, Poland 1936,
Photo by Mietek

Uncle Josef and Aunt Roselle, 1953, Frankfurt

Chapter 8

UNCLE JOSEF AND AUNT ROSELLE

Following an exchange of phone calls from Germany, great jubilation buzzed through our home. My mother explained to Sarah and me that our Uncle Josef was coming to America with his new bride, and they would soon be arriving in Los Angeles. It was 1954, and we were living in the large house next to a church in City Terrace. The plan was for Josef and his wife to sleep on a convertible sofa in the spare room until they could get a place of their own.

I was thrilled at the idea of meeting another actual blood relative—and my father's excitement was contagious. The only other relative I knew was my great-uncle Sol, who viewed our family with disdain and kept us at arm's length. Of course, we had our wonderful surrogate family of survivors, but having a real uncle nearby was something I never thought would actually happen.

As happy as my father was, he was also predictably nervous. After living in barren apartments for four years, he finally decided it was time to furnish our home. He borrowed money and bought enough furniture to fill our house. What an amazing luxury this was. I still remember how every piece looked, and will always associate them with my uncle's arrival. The mahogany furniture was grander than any I had seen in other homes, with the exception of Uncle Sol and Aunt Minnie's.

The dining room table was massive, with chairs upholstered in satin finish and a striped pattern of gold and maroon. In the living room a comfortable sofa and armchairs upholstered in silky brocade surrounded an oval coffee table with leather stretched across the top and gold ornamentation around the concave edges. It had curved legs and gold trim covered the base of each one. To my naïve eyes it was wonderfully elegant. A round cigarette holder and matching ashtray made of textured metal were set on this table. The upright piano stayed against the wall of the living room and still looked brand new. My parents' bedroom was newly furnished in mahogany as well, with matching end tables on either side of the bed. The bed was covered by a quilted satin bedspread and backed by a tall headboard, ornamented in carved wood on each corner.

In the den, which had two walls of windows facing a garden, were a new sofa bed, table, and upholstered chair, and for the bedroom Sarah and I shared, my father bought new but far less lavish furniture. We came home to a twin bed set with quilted cotton bedspreads, a wooden dresser with ample drawers, and a single nightstand between the beds. This seemed to Sarah and me the kind of extravagance rich people enjoyed.

My mother was not a collector of knickknacks, so there were few ornaments in our home, but my father loved vases and had carefully arranged a handsome bronze one in the dining room. Aside from a porcelain lamp painted in a floral design with a silk lampshade, the only other *objets d'art* were elegantly framed photographs taken before the war of Uncle Josef in his "frock and top hat" standing beside Eva, and another photo, framed in gold with an oval inset, of Malka, at the age of sixteen. Also in the room were individually framed photographs of Sarah and me, the ones professionally taken for our immigration identification papers. A framed landscape painting hung over the sofa.

Although Sarah and I knew it was all for the benefit of my father's long-awaited reunion with his brother, we were thrilled to be in these new surroundings after so many years of an almost empty home. My mother had little to say about the new furnishings. She must have known my father went into deep debt to purchase these things.

Uncle Josef in Belgium, 1946

The day they arrived was filled with anticipation and tension. They spoke no English but showered Sarah and me with hugs, kisses, and gifts. Since we rarely received any presents, this was an extraordinary event. They gave me an authentic German dirndl dress with a full skirt, tight bodice, and square neckline, as well as a gold chain necklace with a Star of David pendant. This necklace was the most elegant thing I had ever owned, and I wore it to school every day. While walking home one afternoon, four boys came up behind me, laughing and shouting, and knocked me to the ground. They grabbed my Star of David and pulled it off my neck. City Terrace had a lot of tough kids who ran in gangs and bullied the meeker children like me, and I'll never know if it was an act of anti-Semitism or just plain meanness, but I was distraught. I came home sobbing, humiliated, and hurt, my knees scraped and bleeding, but worst of all, my treasured necklace stolen. My father was sympathetic and furious at the same time. He immediately took me back to look for the boys and the Jewish star, but we found neither. As we searched the sidewalk for the necklace, my father held my hand, walking so fast I could barely keep up. We reported the incident to the school principal, who said he would look into it, but we never heard another word about it.

Uncle Josef and his first wife, Eva

Mietek had a strange love-hate relationship with his brother. After my father died, I found several letters, written in Josef's elegant penmanship, dating to the 1940s. Unfortunately, the letters were in poor condition and parts of them were illegible, but nevertheless I had them translated from Polish into English. From the letters, I was able to glean some sense of what my uncle went through during the war. I learned that although he was able to evade the Germans for quite a while, he was eventually interred in the Bergen-Belsen concentration camp.

Excerpt of post-war letter from Uncle Josef to Mietek

At some point, Josef had discovered that his brother was alive and, like him, had survived the massacre of Jews. Part of one letter reads:

> *I wonder how to start this letter, my dear. Shall I start it with expressing my joy to have my brother alive as the only member of my family who managed to avoid the tragic fate or remembering the tragic events, which we experienced since the time we parted? It is difficult to write all about this in one letter, in which I cry tears of joy and sorrow. . . . I cannot describe in words all that I*

went through, and I would not complain if my sufferings allowed me to feel consoled now that someone more was saved of this hell.

In another letter, Josef explains the torture he had been going through as a concentration camp survivor:

It is nothing compared to the desolation around me. Being lonely without a kindred spirit around me led to my moral breakdown. . . . I have not been able to cry since then. There are no tears in my eyes. My hair has not turned white, but I have gone bald. Everything died inside of me. The two years of slow dying of hunger in the camp could not break me down. Although I lost 39 kilograms [about 85 pounds], I stayed alive, owing to capricious fortune's whims, and to feel the joy of seeing my brother alive. Oh, my dear, you are not a brother to me, but you are a father, mother, wife, and everything that's dearest to me.

After he heard from my father, Josef's letters showed more concern for his brother and also gave some insight into the man my father was before the war. From a letter dated December 27, 1945:

I was afraid that you wouldn't be able to bear being lonely and without help, to which you had been accustomed. I feared for you so much, although I knew you were not threatened by the annihilation to which we fell prey. I was afraid you wouldn't be able to stand the fate of being so far away from home. However, Divine Providence took care of you and, although it left us morally and materially shattered, it kept us alive. Only you and I have survived.

When my uncle was released from Bergen-Belsen after the war ended, he suffered from tuberculosis and was sent to a sanatorium in Brussels. From a letter dated April 2, 1946, he writes:

My only dream now is for us to reunite and pave the way to a new life together. I am reassured by the fact that you are managing to live under such harsh conditions. However, I would not state that you look so great in the photograph that you sent to me. I can see all the pain and suffering you have gone through on your face. And there is not one who can understand you better than I do, my brother. You may have had less physical suffering than I, but you have suffered more spiritual and moral pain, because you have always been more sensitive than I am.

My uncle's letters also mention some of the known history of the Warsaw Ghetto. His wheeler-dealer personality shows through in these communications—he was able to find hiding and provisions for eighty-four people in the middle of the war. He says in one letter that:

Owing to my acquaintances, I managed to protect my family against displacement and I can even say that they were as snug as a bug in a rug. We went to Mila Street . . . [and] built a bunker under the debris. . . . On 19 April, 1943, 84 persons hid in the bunker, which had provisions of food and everything needed for a very long period of time. I, together with nine men . . . stayed on the ground . . . and we were officially deported as the last Jews.

These letters were written just after the war, and describe the Nazi occupation. I often wonder how my uncle could leave his family. In another letter he explains a plan to escape to South America. Although he had no children, Eva and their relatives and servants were left behind in this bunker. He must have known the great danger they were in, but given his remarks, he believed they were safe.

In the summer of 1942, most of the residents of the ghetto were deported to Treblinka for extermination. Many of those remaining resolved to disobey German decrees. Between January and April 1943, a group of underground Jews and Jewish resistance fighters, in preparation for an uprising and to resist deportation, built bunkers and went into hiding. This was the first time the underground organizations showed themselves as an armed force. Weapons were smuggled in; provisions of food, medicine, and even electricity were secreted into shelters built for extended periods of hiding. According to document archives from Yad Vashem, Israel's official memorial to victims of the Holocaust, "The entire population, young and old, were busy creating hiding places, particularly underground. . . . These people, survivors of previous deportations, now prepared everything needed to survive in hiding for months. For around a month, the Jews of the ghetto fought for their lives. Many perished in the fires and smoke of the uprising. Others were murdered in the ghetto streets. Testimonials such as 'Hell has come to Earth' tell us, 'Everything around us is fire! [Whole] streets! I go out into Mila Street . . . all the streets are burning. . . . The entire ghetto is a sea of flames. The ghetto walls are completely surrounded, no one can enter and no one can leave. [The] clothes are burning on people's bodies. Screams of pain and crying, houses and bunkers are burning, everything is in flames.'"

Until I read his letters, I did not know that Josef had taken part in the resistance at the Warsaw Ghetto Uprising on April 19, 1943. It's unbearable to think of him believing his family was "as snug as a bug in a rug" in a horrid bunker—and then to imagine their terrible fate.

After putting down the uprising, German soldiers set fires and burned Mila Street. When my father did speak about the war, he repeatedly told me how members of his family, including the servants, were in hiding and how they all perished at the hands of soldiers. He told me stories of how the maids did things to help the family: kneading bread or slipping away to bakeries and shops to store up on as many goods as they could. When my father spoke of these past events, it was as if he were in a fog, still not believing they had happened. The darkness of my father's voice and the images he recreated of these atrocities—many carried out upon his own flesh and blood—conveyed the stranglehold the past still held on him.

In another letter, my uncle talks about some people he knew who were alive and living in the Polski Hotel. In Warsaw, wealthy Jews went to this hotel to buy foreign affidavits and passports in the hope of leaving for places like Uruguay and Paraguay under new identities. Josef's letter says that the cost was approximately 50,000 zloty per person (about $700,000 in current US dollars). The Jews' identities were to be exchanged with those of German citizens imprisoned by the Allies, but the South American governments did not regard the citizenship papers as authentic and did not honor them. Instead, Jews living in the hotel were deported to the Bergen-Belsen, Auschwitz, and Vittel concentration camps. Some historians now think that the "Hotel Polski Affair" was a German trap to lure rich Jews out of hiding under a false promise of escape.

It's quite possible that Josef bought into this deal but that, like many others, he wound up at Bergen-Belsen until the end of the war. When he got out, Josef weighed 110 pounds.

We didn't know much about Josef's new wife, Roselle, before they arrived in Los Angeles, but it was quite a shock for the family to discover that she was German. After everything that had happened, my parents were now obligated to welcome a German into their home. Not only was she German but she had been married to an SS officer during the war. Roselle flagrantly advertised this fact once they moved in with us. She prominently displayed a photograph of her dead husband, an SS officer, on a shelf in their room. He was in full uniform with a swastika in plain sight.

To my parents' credit, they set aside their personal wounds and reservations, and welcomed both Josef and Roselle with open arms. They were so starved for family, they were willing to overlook almost anything. Perhaps they had already started to forgive the Germans, and being kind to Roselle was one way to move forward. I can't remember either of my parents ever saying anything bad about Germans. I think they were conscious of the fact that hatred breeds more hatred, and did not want their children to grow up with prejudices.

My mother was particularly considerate toward my aunt. Soon after arriving, Roselle often broke down in tears, homesick for Germany and missing her family. To make my aunt feel more at home, my mother put up a Christmas tree during the holidays. This was a one-time occurrence in our family—there had never been Christmas trees before and there weren't any after.

With the little experience we had of Christian holidays, we purchased a few inexpensive ornaments and tinsel to provide what we thought a Christmas tree should look like. It was likely the puniest and most pathetic-looking tree in all of California, but my mother was simply making a sweet attempt to make my aunt feel better. She even invited a priest to the house to speak to her.

Bronia, Ruth, Sarah, 1954, Los Angeles

Sarah and I created a new lexicon with Uncle Josef and Aunt Roselle's arrival. We cleverly asked each other this joke: "Did Josef and Roselle meet in Hamburg and eat frankfurters, or did they meet in Frankfurt and eat hamburgers?" I used to love it when he called her *schatzi*, German for sweetheart. They were a mysterious pair. According to family gossip, Josef and Roselle were involved in black market activities in Germany after the war, and apparently made quite a bit of money. Although I don't know exactly what they had been doing, I was later told it involved prostitution. During the frantic spate of phone calls from Germany, I overheard my parents discussing my uncle's problems. It became urgent that he sail to America as soon as possible because the German police were after him. So my father sponsored his brother as a refugee.

At some point we gave Roselle the nickname Brunhilde, after the vengeful German Valkyrie warrior. We didn't call her that to her face, but that's how we referred to her, a put-down, more for her grandiose stature than a link to her German heritage. I can't remember if my family or some of the other survivor families in our neighborhood created the name, but a German woman, particularly the wife of an SS officer, was never going to be popular in our Polish survivor community so soon after the war.

Plus, my aunt was terribly haughty. She considered herself a fount of knowledge about beauty (maybe she'd picked up valuable experience in this area when she was working with prostitutes), and was always giving my mother tips on how to look and dress better. My mother politely ignored my aunt's suggestions. Instead Mom relied on her ever-present Albolene cream, in its large peach-colored tin, for her beautiful complexion.

While the American dream continued to elude our family, Josef and Brunhilde were able to make the transition from black marketeers in postwar Germany to successful entrepreneurs in Los Angeles without much problem. They came to the United States with lots of cash from sources unknown, and bought a car right away. Even though she didn't know English, Brunhilde found a job at Max Factor, eventually moving to Universal Studios where she was a hair stylist and made wigs for celebrities such as Cher. They started their own wig business in Beverly Hills, importing hair and wigs from Germany. Sarah and I were repulsed by this business, imagining that dead Holocaust victims were keeping them supplied with hair.

Brunhilde's real name, Roselle Friedland, can still be seen on the credits of old television shows like *The Lawrence Welk Show*, *The Carol Burnett Show*, and *Mama's Family*. When I was old enough, I worked for her during summer vacation making ringlets for period-piece wigs. My aunt never paid me for my work, but would treat me to lunch at the Universal Studios' cafeteria, where I could stargaze, spotting idols such as Natalie Wood and Warren Beatty.

Once my uncle and aunt moved to their own place, I always looked forward to visiting them. My aunt bought me a Bauer bike imported from Germany, the country she believed to be the sole source of quality goods. Later, when I married, she gave me a twelve-person dinnerware set of Rosenthal china. Because I didn't send her what she considered to be an appropriate thank-you for this gift, she became angry and told me that she would cut me out of her will. When she died four decades later, I discovered that she had in fact done just that. Ironically, I later had the Rosenthal china appraised, only to discover that it was not really Rosenthal at all, but a cheap knockoff.

Much of my childhood spun around my aunt's dogged campaign to improve my appearance. She insisted that my hair ought to be curly, and gave me one permanent after another, trying to get my hair to look the way she wanted. This felt like torture and I would beg, "Auntie, please stop—it's burning my head." At one point, she gave me four permanents in a row put some curl into my straight hair. They were called Tonis in those days, a brand of toxic-smelling, scalp-frying treatments for girls of all ages. Her efforts finally paid off, as seen in the photo with the Christmas tree. She could feel triumphant that her niece finally had wavy hair. On the other hand, so much talk about what I needed to do to look better crushed my already flimsy self-esteem.

For a while, my aunt repeatedly mentioned adopting one or more of the children in our family, since she was childless. I overheard and even participated in some of these discussions. My mother thought my aunt was out of her mind to even suggest such a thing. She said, "Ruthie, I will never allow it to happen, do you understand?" When it became clear that Sarah would not be adopted, my aunt started up again, this time with the focus on me. I was mortified. Even though my father was impossible to live with, I was not at all interested in the proposition of being adopted out to become my aunt's permanent appearance-improvement project. Although there were many times when I had to escape my father's violence, my mother never once chose to place me with my aunt and uncle. Whether she was afraid that it would be a struggle to get me back from them or whether she simply didn't like or trust my aunt, I'll never know.

Sarah had a boyfriend in high school who was not Jewish, and one day when my father saw him standing on our front porch, he went into a rage. The instant Sarah entered the house, he started screaming insults and then brutally attacked her. He grabbed a stainless steel fork and threw it with so much uncontrollable anger and force that the prongs stuck in the back of her neck. My mother, helpless against my father's temper, sent Sarah to live with my aunt and uncle in West Los Angeles, near Fairfax High School. It lasted for just one semester, after which my father agreed to let her come home to complete high school, and allowed her to stay briefly with the Jackson family in the summer while he tried to cool off over his daughter dating a gentile.

Aunt Roselle, 1954   *Uncle Josef, 1954*

Whenever I conjure up a mental image of Uncle Josef, he is wearing tennis clothes. It seemed he was always dressed and ready for a match. I'm not even sure he actually ever worked, in the traditional sense. Family photos taken after the war show a stylishly dressed Josef, escorting a variety of attractive women despite all he'd been through. Unlike my father, little changed for Josef once he regained his strength in the postwar years, and he found it easy to revert back to a pampered life. Somehow he made it seem like the Warsaw Ghetto, concentration camp, tuberculosis, and black marketeering experiences were just a distant bad memory. It turns out that Josef, like many in my family, suffered from deep depression. His outward appearance, however, never betrayed this secret.

Josef, 1951, Germany

As time went on, my father and uncle fought bitterly. Once, my father borrowed fifty dollars from my uncle, who started asking for the money to be repaid the very next day. Despite his flaws, Josef was a comforting and kind uncle—far nicer to us than Roselle was. He always made us feel special and loved. When Sarah was getting married, Roselle had a wedding shower for her and made a very big deal about the event, which made Sarah uneasy. She didn't like being the center of attention around people she didn't know. My uncle saw the distress on Sarah's face and called her aside.

"What's the matter, honey? You look nervous."

"I am, Uncle. It's too much fuss for me. It makes me uncomfortable."

"Come with me, Sarah. I have something to help you."

Uncle Josef set a glass with brown liquid in front of Sarah. "Here, drink this."

"What is it?"

"It's schnapps, honey, it will make you feel better."

"No, I never drink alcohol. I don't even know what it tastes like."

"Go ahead, it's OK. I promise. You'll feel better."

This wasn't typical for Sarah, but she downed the drink and immediately felt better, appreciating Josef coming to her rescue.

As he got older, my father became obsessed with the family jewelry from Warsaw. He believed that Josef knew where their parents had hidden the treasures and kept insisting that his brother sewed the jewels into the lining of his clothes when he immigrated to the United States. He could never prove this, and my uncle would never admit it, but this scenario became a major theme in my father's later life. He called me every week to rehash and discuss the family jewelry, even though there was no chance that he could ever bring closure to the subject.

Despite their rocky relationship, or maybe because of it, Uncle Josef couldn't stop sobbing at my father's funeral. He was disconsolate even though the two of them fought whenever they spoke and could scarcely tolerate being around each other. Why did the brotherly love described in Josef's letters never manifest itself in the new life they had dreamed of? Was it money? Was it jealousy? Brunhilde? Perhaps it was all of these issues, combined with some deep-seated brokenness in their ability to form and maintain significant relationships.

Gazella and Fred, 1957

Chapter 9

THE TWINS ARRIVE

The summer of 1954 brought some of the happiest memories of my childhood. I remember tranquil, warm days, and spending lots of time with my mother. She seemed the most contented I had ever seen her. She was expecting a baby, and I can still see her, sitting on a blanket under a tree, looking luminously beautiful in a navy blue outfit with a sailor collar that had a white trim. Sunlight peeking through the leaves made her blonde hair shimmer, and her skin was radiant. My mother was especially thrilled to be having another baby after Simon's death.

Late at night on September 30, 1954, I woke up to the sound of voices in the dining room. I knew it wasn't my father, because he was working the night shift at the meatpacking plant. Through the crack in the door I could see Morrie Kingston wearing an overcoat over his pajamas. My mother came rushing out of her bedroom, and the two of them left the house. I heard the front door close. They mistakenly thought they hadn't woken us.

It took me a minute to understand what was happening, but I quickly realized that my mother was going to the hospital to have a baby. Suddenly I was scared, so I jumped out of my bed and crawled into Sarah's. She was sitting straight up in the dark, saying, "Pinch me! Pinch me!" So I pinched her.

"Why did you want me to do that?" I asked.

"Don't you know if you pinch me it means what is happening is not a dream?"

We were excited to know that our mother would soon come home with a brand-new brother or sister, and we couldn't wait to discover which it would be. We were also a little scared of being home alone, so we tried to stay up all night, although we eventually nodded off. When we woke in the morning, Sarah and I were still alone. All day long we worried and wondered about the baby.

My friend Bella, who always seemed to have a direct pipeline to the latest news, gave me the lowdown while we were walking home from school. "Your mother had twins, a boy and a girl," she said, "but the girl has a weird name." My parents had named the twins Frederick and Gazella. Even at the age of eight, Bella was straightforward, not mincing words, and as always, a bit critical. She didn't diminish my excitement one bit.

"I can't believe how lucky we are," I said. "A boy *and* a girl! I can't wait to play with them!"

My father was over the moon with happiness; he finally had a son. He bought a lilac brocade dress with a dark velvet bolero jacket and new shoes for me to wear at Freddy's *bris*, a Jewish circumcision ritual that took place eight days after the twins were born. For the first few weeks, Sarah and I played with our new siblings as if they were dolls. We had a great time dressing them up and rocking them.

At the time of their birth, my mother had been working at Los Angeles County Hospital, training to become first a licensed practical nurse, then a vocational nurse, and then an RN, a fully registered nurse. If I awoke in the night, I would find her sound asleep at the dining room table, head down on top of a pile of chemistry books, nursing texts, and the language books she was reading to improve her English. She went back to work when the twins were six weeks old, and she left them in my care. I was seven, but still remember standing in our dining room in my undershirt and pajama bottoms when she broached the subject.

"Ruthie, I need to talk to you about something."

"OK, Mommy, what's the matter?"

"Do you love the twins, Ruthie?"

"Of course I do. I love them so much!"

"I need you now, so much, to help me. You're a big sister now, and you have to take good care of the babies."

"I always try to, Mommy."

"You do a good job. I see how careful you are with them. So I want to talk to you, because I'm going to go back to work soon. We need the money. It means someone needs to take care of them when I go to work. They're just babies and can't do anything for themselves. I need you to take care of them for me when you get home from school, until I come home from work."

"All right, I think I can do it." I didn't hesitate to agree to do this for two reasons. First, I wanted to please my mother with all my heart, and second, I truly had no idea how grueling it would be to take care of two infants on my own. I knew they had to be fed, and given their vitamins of exactly one smelly liquid teaspoon, and their diapers had to be changed regularly, but beyond that I couldn't comprehend all it entailed.

"You'll have to come right home from school so I can leave for work."

"OK, Mommy. I don't mind taking care of the babies."

My mother's work shift was usually from 3:00 p.m. until 11:00 p.m., but she often worked double shifts when the hospital needed her, in addition to going to school. I could tell that she felt upset about leaving her infants in the care of a school-aged child, but she had no choice. Childcare options were limited then for families who could not afford that. In the early 1950s, no daycare centers existed for tiny babies; mothers were expected to stay home and care for their infants.

Sarah's name did not even enter the conversation. She was four years older and should have been the obvious choice for childcare. But Sarah was studious and already had a social life that took her away from home. She was busy, even if only to watch *American Bandstand*, and skilled at managing to absent herself, well aware that her ticket out was through scholastic achievement. "I was not meant to be a domestic," she once firmly announced to me. Being at home was as torturous for me as it was for her. Yet the age difference seemed to have empowered her. In any case, it became clear to us all that I had to take on the childrearing responsibilities. I never questioned the social order in our family.

So starting in second grade, I came home immediately after school to take care of the twins. My father was home during the day, since he worked the night shift, but he never assumed any of the responsibility for the twins. It was expected that I would also make his dinner and clean the house. Thanks to his job at the meatpacking plant, we always had steak in the freezer, and before he left for work each night, he wanted a full meal, with meat. I would try to stay awake until he went to work, but if I happened to fall asleep, he would wake me, often by slapping me, to make his dinner; it never crossed his mind to cook his own meal. He had been brought up with servants, and expected to be served—even if it meant treating his daughter like a slave. So I made soup and a salad, and cooked steak, green beans, red beets or borscht, and potatoes. He chastised me if the potatoes were not boiled just right—the water had to be at the right level in the pot, completely covering them.

Our home life and our family became extremely chaotic during this period. My father's behavior became progressively worse. With his wife at school or work most of the time, two school-aged daughters, and the addition of two babies, it became normal behavior for him to spend the days screaming, hitting, and throwing tantrums and objects such as glasses or bottles. Often when the twins were still babies, I was the only one around and was on the short end of these antics, but I never got used to his violent episodes. I was stunned whenever minor aggravations set him off, his eyes glazing over with rage. He would mutter curses in Polish, mumblings that would slowly mount in intensity until he was at full roar and waging a one-sided battle against his middle child. Eventually he would leave the room or the house, and I'd cry myself to sleep. In the morning, with eyes swollen and nose stuffy, I'd dutifully feed the babies, then get ready for school.

The poor twins grew up having a child care for them for at least part of the days and nights. Two cribs were placed corner-to-corner against adjacent walls, and I would stand in the center, gently rocking each of the twins' cribs with one hand, ready to jump up whenever my father needed anything. I had morphed into the family servant, a sort of Jewish Cinderella—without the glass slipper, with no Fairy Godmother in sight, and definitely missing a prince, unless you count my father, the self-proclaimed Prince of Poland.

Whatever hopes my aristocratic father might have had for a new career became a distant dream as his mental state began to deteriorate with each passing day. His immigration papers listed his previous occupations as "merchant, photographer, salesman, and furrier," but in America he was employed as a "meat work-man" (the description noted on Gazella's birth certificate) for thirteen years. Lowering himself to this menial level further damaged my father's morale and self-esteem, and he acted out his frustration by feeling superior to others and exhibiting disdain for anyone and anything that didn't meet his prewar standards.

The world was changing around him, but Daddy was stuck in place. When I was about ten, he came home to find my mother and Josef in the kitchen. Enraged that they were together (although there was no evidence of any affair), he ran to get a butcher knife, and in Polish, screamed at Josef, "You are a traitor to our family, and you want my wife. I know how you are, and she is a whore; together I wish the curse of cholera against you. I will kill you even though you are my brother. You are a thief and a traitor!" He damned everyone in sight. In his native culture, the crudest thing you could say to a person was to call them animal names, and he released a long list of invectives involving the body parts of cows, bulls, and pigs. My mother jumped between them to keep Daddy from slashing Josef. With my heart pounding, I ran to the living room and called the police.

The policemen held my father down and called for medical backup, and when the ambulance arrived, two men covered him with a white straitjacket so he could not resist them or get away. But by then he was so quiet it was chilling. He hung his head and I looked away, running to the twins' room, where I stayed for a long time, numb.

When Freddy and Gazella awoke, I dressed them and scur-ried them over to the next-door neighbor's house to play with Dickie and Cindy, two children about the same age. Afterward, my mother went to work just as if it were any other day. Daddy kept calling the house, but my mother wouldn't speak to him and would hand me the phone. He pleaded with me to get my mother to sign the release papers, but she refused.

"Ruthie, please tell her to talk to me," he begged. "Tell her I have to come home. I can't be here anymore. Please, Ruthie, please help me! I love you, and you must help me." This was harder for me than the incident itself. First, because my father couldn't hear, there was no dialogue—all I could say was "Uh-huh" or "Um"—and second, because I was helpless again. Mom left it to me to mediate the situation, and this time I had no one to call for help. Astonishingly, my uncle went to the hospital and signed the papers, claiming he would be responsible for my father. That responsibility was as short lived as a car ride. Josef brought him back to our house and dropped him off, while we waited for the next drama to unfold.

My mother was a mystery to me, particularly where it concerned my father. She explained her passivity by saying she was simply a "European woman," not empowered to resist, fight back, or turn away from her husband—although I knew plenty of other European American women who weren't stuck in abusive relationships. She often tried to leave my father, especially after the twins were born, coming to my room in the night and saying, "We're going! Pack the babies' things and get ready."

One night when the twins were about two years old, she seemed frantic to escape, and I was roused out of bed to help. Still groggy from sleep and certain we were actually leaving this time, I wasn't scared at all. "Mommy, should I pack Gazella's yellow dress?"

Slowly, my mother turned to me. "Go back to sleep, Ruthie," she sighed in a sad, soft voice. "Tomorrow is school."

Gazella was an easy baby and very vocal from the beginning. When she was six weeks old, she began laughing out loud, and Mom came running in from the next room, not believing what she had heard. The laughter must have sounded like music to my forlorn and jaded mother.

Gazella loved to eat, but Freddy was a picky eater and a wild child. Looking back, I would say he fell into the category of incorrigible toddlers. I could not discipline him, and he would not listen to me if I tried to. He was high-strung and hyperactive up until the age of eleven. When he was three, he would imitate my father's behavior by brandishing a steak knife and chasing me around the house. My role was to catch him, take the knife away, and scold him. It wasn't easy catching him, because I was afraid he'd actually stab me. He did stab me once, in the palm of my hand, but fortunately it was with a bobby pin.

Another time, Freddy grabbed the cord of an Italian porcelain lamp and yanked it with all his might. As if it were happening in slow motion, I watched, open-mouthed, as the lamp fell to the floor and shattered. Predictably, I—not Freddy—was punished for letting this happen. My father screamed when he saw the smashed lamp, and accused me of not watching out for things the way I should. He slapped me across the face and shouted, "Clean this up! Do you know how much this cost? Do you know we can't have another one?" Then he started cursing in Polish again, comparing me to any number of animals, and shouting a long stream of accusations peppered with "*Cholera!*" (pronounced Ho-LEH-ra); "*Krowa!*" (kr-OV-a, meaning cow); "*Bitlak! Byk!*" (bull); "*Swiniak!*" (Zv-EEN-i-ak, pig); and "*Kurwa!*" (ku-UR-Va, whore), to name a few.

❧

Freddy didn't get his first haircut until he was three years old. Until then he had beautiful thick, dark, and curly shoulder-length locks. When my dad and Freddy walked into the house after the barbershop visit, my mother and I gasped. Freddy was transformed from a baby boy into a little man. My mother sobbed for days, mourning Freddy's long hair.

My father clearly favored Freddy, his only son and the scion of the Friedland name. He didn't even bother to be subtle about his favoritism. During Hanukkah, for example, all the girls received Hanukkah *gelt* (chocolate candy wrapped to resemble gold coins), while Freddy got a big box filled with toys. Daddy was unfazed by our disappointment.

"The worst dog," he often said, "always gets the biggest bone."

Family dinner, 1954, City Terrace (from left, Roselle, Josef, Sarah, Ruth, Bronia)

Chapter 10

THE SENSATIONAL SEDER

Shortly after the death of baby Simon, the Jewish Welfare Service dropped off a boxed set of Golden Books. The book I remember best was *The Story of Moses*. My parents never read to us, but Sarah could read pretty well by then and she helped me decipher the words and understand the tale. I have vivid memories of the pictures of Moses coming down from Mount Sinai brandishing the Ten Commandments, illustrations of Jews straggling across a parted Red Sea, bushes aflame, and people dancing in reverence to an idol calf. I loved these Golden Books. They probably are responsible for my early sense of identification with Judaism.

The Hebrew Folk School in City Terrace was home away from home for me. From pre-kindergarten through first grade, I was cared for and supervised by the teachers until one of my parents picked me up at the end of the day. Almost all my indoctrination of Judaism came from this place. On Sundays we took more formal classes, and occasionally assemblies were held for families. The rabbi's son was about my age and routinely went around with a small cardboard box collecting nickels for trees to be planted in Israel. He was relentless about those nickels.

Planting an orchard in Israel seemed like a great idea, but a nickel a week was a lot of money back then.

We observed few religious rituals at home, except for lighting *Yahrzeit* candles, but these memorials spooked me. The candles were lit in remembrance of our dead relatives, and my parents went about the house whispering and weeping. My father went to the synagogue in Boyle Heights routinely, either by himself or with other refugee men in our neighborhood, but until Uncle Josef came to live with us, we never made more than token acknowledgements of Hanukkah and Passover. My proudest day in first grade came when I memorized the Four Questions for the Passover seder.

Some of our neighboring families kept kosher and were more religious than mine. Still, I strongly identified with Judaism. It gave me a feeling of warmth and belonging even though my mother had lost her faith after the war and couldn't have cared less about religious rituals. This always bothered and confused me, because she was proud that her father had been a Talmudic scholar, and told me stories about his intelligence regarding Jewish theology and cultural life. Reflections about her family both saddened us and invariably opened sensitive wounds about the heartbreak of being born into a Jewish family.

When I was thirteen, my father told me to "dress up" and go with him to the Yom Kippur services at the temple. Yom Kippur is the Day of Atonement for Jews. The evening begins with singing the slow, rhapsodic, lyrical *Kol Nidre* (also known as "all vows") and concludes at the next day's dusk with blowing the *shofar*, a ram's horn, to announce the end of fasting. I was thrilled, but the problem was that my only shoes were school shoes, brown penny loafers, and a pair of worn-down flip-flops (or "zories"). Of course neither seemed appropriate for this auspicious occasion. Excitedly, I borrowed a pair of nice shoes with kitten heels from Sarah, and ran to catch up to my father on the street, shuffling along in these shoes that were several sizes too big. Still, they made me look appropriately sophisticated, or so I thought. My father turned to see me hustling up next to him and suddenly became unhinged. He smacked me across the face.

"Go home, Ruthie!" he shouted. "I don't want to be seen with you. You look like a stupid whore. I won't take you to *shul* looking like a stupid whore."

I was mortified. I had tried so hard to please him. I wasn't even sure what he meant by "stupid whore," but I knew it was a barbed insult. It's what he often called my mother when he was angry with her. I returned to the house sobbing and told my mother what happened. Her face hardened at my humiliation.

"He's a hypocrite," she responded. "A sinful hypocrite."

That night I cried myself to sleep, feeling rejected and disappointed for not being able to attend the service. All I'd wanted was to be part of something beautiful, part of a cathartic experience that faith, song, and prayer could provide.

A year later, my mother, always the dutiful nurse, had to work during the first night of Passover, so I was responsible for making my family's Passover seder. By this time, Sarah had graduated from high school and was away at college, so I was in charge.

My mother had showed me everything I needed to know to make the perfect seder, and I spent the whole day preparing—matzo ball soup, gefilte fish, brisket prepared in a pressure cooker. I was most concerned about the texture of the matzo balls—they must not be too hard or too mushy—and I made sure the bitter herb, green vegetable, lamb shank, hard-boiled egg, *charoset*, and matzo were properly placed on the Passover plate. I set the table using the best dishes we had.

My father had to buy new drinking glasses, which happened routinely in our house, since he would have to replace the ones he threw against the wall in one of his rages. We only had drinking glasses on hand when he purchased new ones whenever company was joining us for dinner. With my mother and Sarah away, our seder consisted of my father, Josef, Roselle, the seven-year-old twins, and me. I should have realized a nice, normal family dinner was not likely with my father in attendance, but somehow I was always optimistic he would behave himself.

Usually the youngest person present asks the Four Questions as part of the Passover seder ritual, which starts with (in Hebrew), "Why is this night different from all other nights?" I was looking forward to asking the questions, even though I wasn't the youngest. I was, however, the youngest there who knew how to recite them in Hebrew, and I imagined my uncle being impressed by my Hebrew, praising me for my abilities. I couldn't wait for my opportunity to perform.

Freddy wasn't wearing a *yarmulke*, a traditional Jewish skullcap, at the table. He had never been to religious school, so he wasn't versed in Jewish laws and traditions. My father chose odd times to be religious, and this was one of those times.

"Fredjek, where is your *yarmulke*?" my father demanded.

"I don't know. I don't need it," my brother offhandedly replied.

"You must have your head covered. I'll find something for you to wear."

My father came back with a big Panama hat for him to wear, but Freddy was having none of it. He pulled it off his head.

"Put the hat back on your head and stop this." I could see my father seething, but as a typical seven-year-old, Freddy refused to wear the hat.

"Put on the hat, now!" my father bellowed at him. Freddy became defiant and just kept shaking his head.

My father's rage grew more intense until he shouted the dreaded word *pasak*, or belt. Whenever I heard that word, my stomach knotted. I was never prepared when my father whipped off his belt, and I certainly didn't expect it on Passover.

The *pasak* came off, and my father started beating Freddy relentlessly right there at the table. Freddy was beet red, crying and screaming as my father whipped him across his chest. My uncle and aunt pleaded with my father to stop the beating.

"Stop it right now!" Josef shouted. "You're an animal. Stop it now!"

Everyone at the table held their breath to see how my father would react to the worst Polish insult you could receive. But he was unfazed, crazed—in fact animalistic. He continued the abuse, smacking Freddy's body with the belt even more viciously than before. Freddy screamed louder, getting redder by the second. Crimson welts erupted on his skin.

Furious that my father wouldn't listen to their pleas, my aunt and uncle got up and left. I wanted them to stay and protect me, Gazella, and Freddy, or to take us with them. They were the only sensible adults present, and we certainly wouldn't be able to calm Daddy down.

Their exit pulled a dangerous trigger. As soon as my aunt and uncle walked out the door, my father grabbed the tablecloth and pulled as hard as he could, the way a magician might do. The table settings I had carefully laid out flew through the air and crashed to the floor. All the food I had so painstakingly cooked was wasted, lying in heaps around the room. No one had a chance to eat one bite. And needless to say, we were again without drinking glasses in the Friedland household.

My father ran out of the house and didn't come back that night. When my mother came home after work, I told her what had happened, but she didn't say a word. She made us some tea and cinnamon toast, and the two of us sat in silence. It struck me as incongruous—we were sitting there eating leavened bread, which is forbidden during Passover, yet Freddy had been beaten to a pulp for not wearing a *yarmulke*. It all seemed so random and capricious. I began to appreciate why my mother was not observant. For once I fully understood when she mouthed the word "hypocrite" about her husband. We were supposed to have been celebrating our blessings as a family, because as Jews we were finally free from oppression. Hardly. Our family, I realized, was never going to be normal, no matter how hard we tried.

Ruth, at the Kwapishes' home, 1957

Chapter 11

MEMORIES

I have been blessed—or some might say cursed—with an excellent memory and can recall details from long ago. As I look back, memories from my childhood and adolescence continue to bombard me. They are mixed together as both good and bad, but the upsetting memories, because they were so traumatic, stand out more. My father's mental condition and our home life continued to deteriorate as the twins grew older. I knew the police station number by heart from all the times I had called. Sometimes the officers calmed him down, but at other times they took him away to a psychiatric ward of a hospital. Mostly we just had to deal with him as best we could.

Looking at old photographs, I notice a distinct change in lifestyle from before the twins were born, and the one after. In the pre-twins photos, Sarah and I are riding bikes, skating, and at the beach. My mother looks serene and Rubenesque. But I rarely find a photo of my mother in the post-twins era. Her responsibilities had doubled and she was still the major bread-winner in the family. Gone are pictures of Sarah and me being kids, in part because Sarah was eleven years old when the twins were born, and because she tried to distance herself from our soul-crushing household. And as the twins' nanny, the family housekeeper, and cook, I no longer had time for simple childhood activities.

My piano teachers were the lifeline that kept me afloat amid looming abuse. One night when I was five or six, our new teacher, a former student from the Los Angeles Conservatory of Music, took Sarah and me to the opera to see *Hansel and Gretel*. I still remember the lush scenery of the stage and the beautiful singing and costumes—it was a great spectacle.

I had assumed that all the children in our refugee circle took music lessons, but I was mistaken. In fact, I was the only one who kept playing over the years. Whenever the Kingstons and Jacksons came to our house, it was my job to entertain them with a concert, and I performed Beethoven, Schumann, Schubert, Brahms, Liszt, and Debussy. The Kingstons later got a piano. "So," they told their daughter, "you can play like Ruthie."

My mother found teachers for Sarah and me wherever we moved, and I remember one teacher, Mrs. Thurman, who came to our house to give lessons. On her first day, the twins were bouncing in their playpen in the center of the living room, creating an impish distraction. When Mrs. Thurman sat down beside me on the piano bench, a large garter snake slithered out from behind the piano. She spied the snake slinking toward her and shrieked like a banshee, running out of the house. Sarah and I never saw her again.

Even without the snake, our house always pulsed with commotion. Freddy liked to keep rhythm with the music, chirping little noises as he held on to the playpen and bounced against the railing. Although it was not the best environment for practicing, Sarah and I somehow managed to stay focused.

My mother found a new piano teacher in San Marino. Her house was the epitome of California style in those days, complete with a sunken living room, mirrors everywhere, and a French poodle. Everything was shiny, including the teacher. She wore gold lamé shoes and black skintight pants, and had big, platinum-blonde hair teased to oblivion. Even at the age of eight, I thought something was odd about the way she dressed for a piano lesson. I felt so ill at ease in her house among the gleaming opulence that I told my parents I would rather they find me another teacher.

Gilda Grego, who trained and taught at the Los Angeles Conservatory, was one of the most important teachers we had. She was tall, slender, and always dressed the same way: straight black skirt and white shirt. Miss Grego was our teacher for the duration of high school, and although she looked stern and seldom smiled, she was patient and helped me correct my playing. Sarah thought she was mean, because she was so demanding, but among other things Miss Grego taught me the importance of music in the Catholic church. Until I met her, I did not know what a monk was or the significance of a Gregorian Mass. She charged ten dollars for a one-hour lesson, which seemed exorbitant at the time, and I don't know how my mother found the money to pay her, but she did.

One day when Sarah and I walked to a music store in Alhambra to buy the sheet music for *Moonlight Sonata,* we babbled about the music we wanted to learn, about our piano lessons, and how grand it would feel to be a concert pianist.

"Won't it be wonderful to just be able to play the piano all the time?" I said.

"But you have to practice *so much!*"

"I don't care, I love it. Just think of all the music we'll know by heart!"

As the years went by, we continued our long walks every week to our teacher's studio, stretching them out for as long as possible to avoid being at home. Sarah spoke intensely about her hopes for living a great life, and when discussing our father, she would say, resignedly, "Daddy's crazy, and there's not much we can do about it."

Miss Grego chastised my mother for not providing us with a radio or record player to listen to good music. Duly admonished, my mother bought a radio for our house, and sometime later even found the funds to buy a record player. Sarah and I were ecstatic—a whole unexplored world opened up to us, and we constantly listened to a wide variety of music, including Marian Anderson, an American-born singer who performed and recorded operas, arias, and traditional spirituals and who was the first black artist to perform at the Metropolitan Opera in New York in 1955. She won many awards, including the National Medal of Arts and the 1991 Grammy Lifetime Achievement Award, and eventually participated in the civil rights movement in the 1960s. We also had a recording of Harry Belafonte singing "The Click Song," a traditional song of South Africa, with Miriam Makeba. (Years later I was able to take my mother to a Harry Belafonte concert in Berkeley, where he introduced his latest protégé, Greek singer Nana Mouskouri. It was a transcendent experience for my mother, and I remember the joy of watching her—smiling broadly, completely relaxed and transported for an hour or two to a place free of worry or responsibility.)

When I became a piano teacher, the first thing I told parents was to be sure their young children listened to great singing. I mentioned some of my favorite recordings, along with music from *Hansel and Gretel* and *The Magic Flute*. As a graduate student I assisted the choral director of the children's choir at Indiana University in a performance of Benjamin Britten's *War Requiem*. The final production was a stunning success, and extremely rewarding to hear and see the young, often rambunctious, children commit to a polished performance.

Although purchasing a piano, a radio, and a record player placed financial hardship on my parents, it changed my life. For everything my parents, especially my father, took away from us, I have to give them credit for sacrificing other things so we could have music. Somehow they wisely realized that music was a gift I could hold on to forever.

Aunt Roselle, Ruth, and Queenie, 1954, Los Angeles

I came home from school one day and was surprised by the arrival of Queenie, who I assumed my parents bought just for me. She had a shiny coat of soft black hair and floppy ears—an American cocker spaniel mix—and we named her after the 1950s TV show, *Queen for a Day*. On this program, run-of-the-mill, usually downtrodden women would discuss their particular tales of woe, and the studio audience voted for the one they deemed "Queen for a Day." Weeping with joy, the winner would be draped in an ermine-collared cloak and a rhinestone tiara, handed a bouquet of flowers, and bestowed some other major gift such as a sofa-loveseat combo or a color TV. My aunt always told me I ought to go on the show and ask for a washer and dryer for my mother, but I didn't think I could sway the audience with my sob story.

Of course, I was very excited about Queenie and couldn't wait to play with her every day after school. One night, however, a major obstacle stood in my way: I had to eat the liver we had for supper before I was allowed to play with the puppy. My parents had suffered terrible hunger during the war and couldn't understand why I didn't want to eat when food was available.

I remember sitting at our kitchen table, watching my mother cut up the liver into tiny pieces. All I could think about was playing with the puppy, and I kept repeating to my parents that I couldn't eat the liver because it looked as appetizing as an old shoe. My father lost his temper, took off his dreaded belt, and started beating me. I tried to eat the liver, rocking back and forth in my chair to dodge the belt, but somehow I lost my balance and cut my mouth on the metal side of the table. My parents were screaming, I was crying and drooling blood, and chunks of liver lay spattered across the table and floor. My ever-practical mother, who kept penicillin in the refrigerator, ran over and jabbed me with a shot to ward off infection. The only good part of this whole ordeal was when it was all over, and I still hadn't eaten any liver.

In the fourth or fifth grade at Grandview Elementary in Monterey Park, the school nurse weighed me and said I was overweight. I didn't really believe her until the kids at school started calling me

"Ruth, Ruth, the big fat telephone booth." In a photo of me, the twins, Aunt Roselle, and Sarah, I appear as a normal, slightly pudgy little girl. When the nurse asked me what I ate when I got home from school, I lied and said half a sandwich and an apple. She advised me to leave off the sandwich.

Clockwise from left, Sarah, Aunt Roselle, Ruth, and the twins, 1955

The truth was, we rarely had a proper dinner so I ate whatever I could find when I got home. Often there was no food in our house to make dinner for the twins, so I would scrounge around to find some tuna or eggs. When my mother had a day off from work, she made a big pot of noodles with farmer cheese, cinnamon, and sugar. My father always managed to have a stash of bakery rye bread, which was supposed to be saved exclusively for him, but I sometimes surreptitiously raided his coffers and crammed as much of it as I could into my mouth, along with his herring, anchovy paste, or lox. Whenever he found out, he would get angry and punish me for eating his provisions. In my defense, I was hungry. I loved these foods and often decided whatever penance was in store for me was worth the risk. I also discovered the enticement of candy bars, and whenever my mother sent me to the store to buy a pack of cigarettes and Albolene cream, I'd buy a candy bar or two for my troubles.

As I grew into adolescence, I slimmed down and learned how to subsist on Jell-O and popcorn, often for weeks at a time. Berkeley High School had an open campus, so at lunchtime I walked a few blocks to Woolworth's and bought a bag of popcorn for ten cents. On other days, I went to The Pantry, a nearby coffee and pastry shop on Shattuck Avenue, and splurged on a muffin or cookie, but it was too expensive to become a habit.

Our house on Graylock Avenue (photo taken in 2009, with the big trees gone)

After the twins were born, we moved east from City Terrace to Graylock Avenue in Monterey Park. With its $11,000 price tag, this was the first house my parents owned, and I spent a good part of my childhood there. My mother always commented that the street was given a glum name for a reason—everyone who lived there seemed to have problems. My dysfunctional family fit right in.

I remember sitting in the backyard, under the cool shade of a green-and-white-striped aluminum awning my uncle had bought for us. While keeping a watchful eye on the twins playing on the lawn, I'd be thinking, "I'd give anything to be someone else." When my teacher Mr. McCormick called my mother in to school to meet with him, she worried that it had to do with my behavior.

"Does she do something wrong in class?"

"No, Ruth is a good student. Her grades and her work at school are excellent."

"What is the matter?" My mother was clearly confused.

Mr. McCormick hesitated. "I'm not sure exactly how to say this, but Ruth appears to be a morose child. She seems sad, distant, and detached, and I was wondering if there's something I should know so I can be of help to her?"

With her voice slightly quivering from nervousness and the inability to respond properly, my mother said, "No, Mr. McCormick. Thank you for paying attention to Ruthie, but everything is fine. Just fine."

She had no idea what *morose* means, but she didn't want to admit that to my teacher. She politely left and chose to ignore what Mr. McCormick had to say. When she got home, I overheard her discussing the conference with Sarah, who explained the meaning of morose. They had a good chuckle over the English barrier keeping my mother in the dark.

Sarah and my mother had a different type of bond. When it came to issues about me, they teamed together not so much as mother and daughter but as equals, with me being treated as the child. Puberty came early for me and I remember my mother and Sarah being amused over this new version of me. It didn't occur to them to discuss any of these changes with me, and I was left on my own to figure out what to do. I had to turn to the school nurse for questions and instructions, which seems strange since my mother was a nurse and would have been an expert on educating me about early adolescence. I now appreciate how Mr. McCormick cared enough to try to discover why I was so glum. Of course, he had no way of knowing about all my responsibilities at home, and about my father's epic eruptions. My teacher just saw me as a sad third grader.

My memory of those years primarily consists of taking care of the twins, waiting for my mother to come home from her shift at the hospital, often around midnight, hating my father, fighting with Sarah, and trying to keep company with our dismal group of neighbors. I tried to express my feelings to my mother.

"I hate him so much."

"Ruthie, there are families who have it much worse than you," she'd say knowingly from her experience in emergency rooms. (She worked in all units of the hospital—maternity, surgery, internal medicine, pediatrics, and emergency care—as she continued to earn higher levels of nursing degrees.) She never divulged what she saw, only to say it was shocking and revolting. This offered little solace for me—I found no comfort in discovering that other children were being beaten even more severely than I.

I was overly empathetic, and trembled every time I heard a siren. I cried easily when I learned about children who never returned to school because they had contracted polio or died from leukemia. Our neighbors also helped me realize that the Friedlands were not the only family with inordinate burdens. I could walk down Graylock Avenue and mentally tick off the problems of the inhabitants in each home.

Right next door lived a family with a twenty-year-old boy, Bob, who had the intellectual capacity of a seven-year-old. Daddy was very kind to him and would play piggyback, hoisting him up on his shoulders even though he probably weighed at least fifty pounds more than my father. Across the street was another family with a developmentally delayed (known as retarded in those days) daughter. At the top of the hill up the street lived a woman who had oral cancer and returned from the hospital without a tongue. She terrified me, and I had nightmares about getting my own tongue cut out. This woman lived only a couple of agonizing months after the surgery.

A family across the street had a boy with leukemia who over time relapsed and was in and out of the hospital. One day my father went to their house to carry him (he was about eighteen years old and weighed almost nothing) to a waiting ambulance. My father wanted him to see a familiar face just before his final ride to the hospital. He came home with tears in his eyes as the boy was taken to die in the same hospital where my mother worked.

My parents had a lot of compassion for the troubles of our neighbors, but their own problems were vocalized louder than anyone else's on the block. The neighbors were privy to my father's tirades, and one such rant was actually kind of funny. My mom was cleaning the stove in preparation for Thanksgiving, and as she pulled the oven away from the wall, gas suddenly leaked out and burst into flames. She poured water on it—which was the exact wrong plan, because it caused the flames to shoot even higher into the kitchen. And my dad, who had been asleep, jumped out of bed and ran onto the front porch in his boxer shorts, yelping at the top of his lungs in his pronounced Polish accent, "NEIGHBORS, FIRE! NEIGHBORS, FIRE! NEIGHBORS, FIRE!" No one paid any attention to his screaming, thinking it was just another of his outbursts. Soon the fire trucks rolled in and for what seemed like the hundredth time, I wrapped up the twins and took them next door for safety. Once my mother was assured we were all OK, she ran back inside to retrieve the only material things important to her—her naturalization papers and her nursing certificates. Nothing else mattered to her as much as those documents.

⁓

I revisited Monterey Park in April 2009 and, remarkably, the green-and-white-striped awning from Uncle Josef still hung over the porch. The clothesline I had used every day to hang up the twins' diapers was no longer there, and the incinerator, later outlawed by city code, had been replaced with a handsome brick barbeque. A plague of insects or something similar must have attacked the neighborhood, because the street was denuded of the leafy trees that once stood tall in front of the homes we all lived in.

Revisiting Graylock Avenue brought back memories: riding my bike on Mom's day off, going to the bookmobile to get Nancy Drew books, and later to the library, which seemed as if it were miles away, setting out to read the classics. My mother's love for Yiddish literature and theater—stories by Sholem Aleichem, I.J. and B.J. Singer—had spread to me, and when I recently saw a production in New York's Yiddish Theater called *Shlemiel the First*, I longed for her to be with me to enjoy it.

But revisiting Graylock Avenue also brought back the traumas. Sarah had scads of friends, several of whom had been banned from our house because they were not Jewish. Daddy would rudely drive them off whenever they stopped by, especially if they were males. Both Sarah and I learned never to bring anyone home, even to the front porch, for fear that Daddy would create a scene. And after we left City Terrace and the Hebrew Folk School, Sarah turned away from Judaism. She joined Job's Daughters, went on trips and outings with other members, immersed herself in their customs and lifestyle, even celebrating with them on holidays, and sang songs such as "Onward Christian Soldiers."

Even the nurses who occasionally gave my mother a ride home from work late at night were never invited in. One exception was the Polish-Catholic Kwapish family, with their daughters Diane, the older one, and Jessica, who was just a little older than I and already an accomplished ballet dancer. Mr. and Mrs. Kwapish had a car even in 1950, and my parents bonded with them. We visited each other's home frequently, and for some reason my father never lost his cool around this family. This friendship lasted for many years, until Mrs. Kwapish died of cancer. I went to their home with my parents just before she died, but I wasn't allowed into her darkened bedroom, so I nervously sat in the living room and waited for my parents. Her husband, who my mother always called an "angel," no longer visited us after his wife's death.

⌒

On Graylock Avenue we always kept the outside gate locked so the twins could not escape. When they did, they inevitably took off in opposite directions, and I had to chase them all over the neighborhood. Ditto for our dog Dotsie, who Sarah had brought home from college one day—a new puppy for my mother and me. We named her Dotsie for her black and white spots, and I loved playing with her and her puppies. Sometimes when my father was angry he took it out on Dotsie, tormenting and beating her. I could hear her whining and crying, and I wondered how anyone could do this to an innocent, sweet dog. When I went back to see the house, my first thought when I looked at the garage was of poor abused Dotsie.

⌒

A torture technique my father learned in the Russian prison was turning lights on and off continuously during the night. When he wasn't working the night shift, he would do this in my room all night long, and many days I went to school exhausted and bleary-eyed after a sleepless night. This behavior was intended to harass my mother, since she slept in my room most nights when he was home.

After the horrifying incident of my finding my father and baby Fred lying on my parents' bed with bags over their heads, my father was taken away to the psychiatric ward at LA County Hospital. He was away for much longer this time and would call home daily, pleading for me to have him released. Feeling sorry for him, I slipped away and rode the bus alone to visit him at the hospital. A nurse accompanied me to his room. The whole environment in the psychiatric unit was bizarre and creepy—heavy, sobering silence punctuated by sudden outbursts of screams and shrieks. When I walked into his room, he looked at me but said very little. His speech was slurred and I couldn't tell if he had been sleeping or if he couldn't hear anything without his hearing aid; perhaps he was medicated or had already been given shock treatment. My father was not in a private room, and nurses were fluttering in and out with medications, asking other patients questions I couldn't understand.

Antipsychotic drugs were first introduced in the 1950s, but I don't know if they were used to treat my father. Few drugs were available and most were used for long-term institutionalized patients. On the few occasions when he received electric shock treatments, it did very little to improve his condition. He always believed that everyone around him was crazy and that he was the only sane person present. He still spoke about these treatments well into old age, claiming they permanently damaged him. Even in his eighties, he blamed everyone for being against him.

During one of my visits I remember hanging around for a while, observing him and the things going on around him. Before leaving, I leaned close to his face to say good-bye, and with startling coherence, he popped open his eyes and asked, "How's Mommy?"

My parents became naturalized citizens on April 4, 1958. Although their declaration of intention was dated April 3, 1952, it required at least five years of residency and examinations. They both studied for the mandatory test, but my mother really crammed. She was nervous, afraid she would not pass, but equally determined to become a US citizen. I remember the day they returned home from the federal courthouse after being sworn in. My mother was overjoyed—both she and Daddy had passed and received their citizenship. "Ruthie, I was so nervous when I was interviewed by the judge. He asked me, 'Who was the Father of this country?' I knew the answer! 'George Washington,' I told him. This brought a big smile to his face!" Their new American names appeared on their naturalization papers: my father was now Michael Friedland and my mother was Broniz Friedland. Sarah and I were also US citizens, but because we were under the age of sixteen, we were not required to appear in court. My mother's excitement was contagious as we all hugged each other. By now my father had retreated to another room. He was too exhausted or overwhelmed to celebrate, but delighted with his new name.

ᵔ‿ᵔ

My father was jealous about anything to do with my mother, always thinking she was sleeping with the doctors at the hospital. He went so far as to accuse her of having a hemorrhoidectomy because she was in love with the surgeon. After all, nothing generates sexual passion as much as having one's hemorrhoids surgically excised.

As Sarah and I reached adolescence, the realization that he couldn't totally control us anymore was too much for him. He started adding new household rules to make himself feel more important, including one very strange edict: we were forbidden from closing the door when we used the bathroom. We had no idea why, but it was a humiliating invasion of privacy for an adolescent girl. My solution to this problem was to use the bathroom at school, and just hold it at home.

One particularly harrowing episode of his maniacal behavior happened while practicing the piano when I was thirteen years old and in the eighth grade in junior high. He started beating me with a belt, and I'll never know what caused him to get worked up into this frenzy. He eventually grabbed me, ripping my shirt off while I sat on the piano bench. Embarrassed, naked, and scared, I ran over to the window and clung to the drapes, screaming, sobbing, and dodging his blows. I was clutching the drapes so hard, I pulled them down—hooks, rod, and all—hardware and fabric heaped all over the living room. My mother was home but didn't get directly involved except to tell me to get ready to go. Next thing I knew, the doorbell rang and my guidance counselor from school, Mrs. Seawell, was at the front door. I was shocked to see her. My mother handed me a paper bag she had hastily packed with some of my things, and sweet Mrs. Seawell took me for a root beer float. I stayed with her all summer in her home in San Pedro. She even gave me her daughter's clothes to wear. Escaping from my family became a frequent pattern in my adolescence.

Sarah, Ruth, and our bows, 1950,
Los Angeles

Almost every photo of Sarah and me as a child includes the ubiquitous bow. I honestly think my mother made me wear them until I went to high school. It was embarrassing, especially as I got older, because the bows set me apart from my classmates. I know now it was one of my mother's ways of showing affection, but it was a European custom and it made me feel out of place.

By the time I was in junior high, she started pulling my long hair straight back away from my face, securing it in place with a ribbon. One summer, Mr. Lincoln, a teacher at my school, came to our house selling encyclopedias door-to-door. Knowing he might soon be my teacher, my mother thought it would be rude not to invite him in. He went through his whole sales pitch about the educational advantages of having a new set of encyclopedias, and as he wound down his spiel, my mother thanked him but said she was not interested in buying the books. Our family really couldn't afford to spend money on such luxury items.

A few months later, as luck would have it, I was assigned to Mr. Lincoln's homeroom, and one day he called me to his desk at the end of the period. He eyed me cruelly, focusing on my tight ponytail. "You resemble a peeled onion," he said. I fought back tears and went straight to the girl's bathroom where I took a hard look at my face in the mirror.

Sarah and Ruth, Russian River, California, 1968

I was not at all popular in junior high, but at the end of the year, the school paper named students who had been awarded accolades—such as Best Couple, Best Dancer, Most Likely to

Succeed, Best Dresser. All of a sudden, I spotted my name next to the Best Hairdo accolade. I hadn't realized anyone, except for a couple of close friends, even knew my name.

Auntie Roselle, a.k.a. Brunhilde, visited us on Graylock Avenue often and routinely cut my hair. Of even more concern than my hair to her was my nose. She became obsessed with her desire for me to have plastic surgery, so my nose wouldn't look so Jewish.

"Ruthie, I'll make you a wonderful sweet-sixteen party if you have your nose fixed," she declared. "You'll see, you'll look beautiful for the party. I'll buy you a new outfit and I'll fix your hair."

"No, Auntie, I don't want an operation."

"You will have the best party. I can invite the Lennon Sisters from the *Lawrence Welk Show* to your party. All your friends will be jealous."

"Auntie, I don't want a party. I don't want a nose job. And I don't have any friends to invite to the party."

"Ruthie, you'll be as pretty as Uncle Sol's granddaughter Susan. Your nose will be cute and your face will look so much better."

"Auntie, I don't want a nose job, and I don't want a party. Please stop."

I was a big disappointment to her. I passed on not only the new nose, but also the big celebrity bash and the envy of all the friends I didn't have.

⁂

One of my happiest memories is of a surprise party for my fourteenth birthday, thrown by my mother and Sarah. I had never had a surprise party before, and I couldn't believe my good fortune. The Jackson and Kingston families were there, and the table was laid out with cake and ice cream. For a gift, my parents gave me a Singer sewing machine, which meant I could finally create my own wardrobe.

My father, always the dapper dresser, had taught me to love fashion, especially expensive, quality clothes, and as much as I longed for stylish clothes, I couldn't afford them. I wore the same skirt and blouse nearly every day and washed them each night. Until I was given the sewing machine, my clothes were all hand-me-downs or the cheapest choices from Newberry's, a now-defunct five-and-dime-type store in our neighborhood. I started babysitting to earn money to buy fabric and Vogue patterns for my school clothes. Finally I'd have some nice clothes to wear.

I'm not sure how I was able to fit it in, but I took a weekend job when I was about fifteen, cleaning house for a couple who wrote for the *Perry Mason* show. It took me two-and-a-half hours to get to their house by bus, and then I worked all day on Saturday. They would leave the week's dishes piled in the sink, as well as a week's worth of laundry. Their daughter, who was only two years older than I, practiced her violin while I hung up her clothes. I was proud to earn some money, and thought I'd be able to keep it as spending money, but my father had a different idea. When he saw what I was earning, he demanded I give him all my wages, which he promptly used toward car payments.

Much later, when I stopped speaking to my father for years, Cesia Kingston begged me to let the past go, proclaiming that "A father is a father." I'm not sure she fully understood the baggage that came with "father" in our house, but after our talk I sat at my desk and composed a letter to Cesia, tactfully explaining why I could not associate with him any longer. I read it over many times, but in the end I could not bring myself to send it. If I sent it, questions would arise, ones I wasn't prepared to answer. I would have to describe how we had suffered at his hands, and I hesitated to break the link of secrets in our family. I didn't want Cesia to think I was made of stone—of course I had feelings of love. But it was an opaque, messy, sporadic kind of love—an aberration of the emotions most women feel toward their fathers.

Cesia would not have understood. In our community, being a survivor trumped everything. It even trumped being a tyrant.

Sarah in City Terrace, 1951

Chapter 12

MY SISTER, SARAH

Sarah had a profound influence on me throughout my life.
Busy with extracurricular activities, learning French, and
participating in debate teams and public speaking events for
which she won many awards, she always seemed to be repre-
senting her school at some important competition. On top of our
piano was a line of trophies she had won, and they soon spilled
over onto the shelves in our bedroom. In high school, she was
chosen to attend Northwestern University for a summer session
of public speaking; I remember going to Union Station in down-
town Los Angeles to see her off. I was in awe—first, I had never
been to a train station before and this one was quite impressive.
Second, the letters she wrote home told of the wonderful family
she was living with and the many new friends she was making.
I wasn't envious, but it struck me how different our lives were,
even though we were such close sisters.

When her interests began broadening, she became more
sensitive to the four-year gap in our ages and viewed me as the
little sister who was in her way much of the time. I couldn't help
feeling hurt and left out when she would say, "Ruthie, leave me
alone. You can get home from school on your own now. I want
to enjoy my time with my friends."

On the other hand, when it was just the two of us at home, she was 100 percent my kindred spirit. We waited up for our mother to come home from work at midnight, and although we were exhausted, we baked sugar cookies or found things to do to stay awake. One night a huge spider crept into the house, terrorizing us. We scrambled up onto the kitchen counter and sat holding each other, terrified that the spider would somehow find and attack us before our mother got home.

Throughout our childhoods, Sarah and I shared the chronic background noise of dread and anxiety permeating our household. We were somehow united by the constant chaos of our parents' stormy relationship and the need to dodge Daddy's mercurial temper.

Sarah taught me how to dance. The record player was in our parents' bedroom, and when Daddy was asleep in the den or out of the house, she played the 45-rpm recordings popular at the time, such as "Get a Job" (The Silhouettes), "At the Hop" (Danny & the Juniors), and "Rockin' Robin" (Bobby Day). She twirled me under her arm, rolling me next to her, and then swinging me out again. I didn't have Sarah's natural grace, and it took more than a few attempts to master the steps, but we would burst into laughter from so much fun. She would trot back over to the record player, lift the arm, and drop the needle down on the same song, encouraging me to try again until I got it. She also taught me The Bop, which she had learned either at school dances or from TV shows. I thought my big sister was the height of coolness. Rock 'n' roll was just beginning in 1959, and she wept when she learned that an airplane carrying Buddy Holly and Ritchie Valens had crashed, killing them both.

Nearly everyone we knew from the City Terrace crowd came to hear Sarah give her high school valedictory address, titled, "What America Means to Me." She practiced the speech so much at home that now, decades later, I still remember parts of it. To explain her feelings about America, she used the metaphor of a key unlocking the door to freedom. She also quoted from "The New Colossus," the poem by Emma Lazarus that welcomed the millions of immigrants pouring in through Ellis Island and the port of New York. This poem was engraved on a bronze plaque and mounted inside the lower level of the pedestal of the Statue of Liberty: "Give me your tired, your poor, / Your huddled masses, yearning to breathe free."

For our community of survivors who had outlived the horrors of World War II, Sarah's speech was transformational. The symbolism of her graduating first in her class was apparent to everyone. She represented what could be accomplished in America, and every person in our refugee community shed tears as they listened to her valedictory.

It was no surprise to anyone when, during her senior year of high school, Sarah was accepted to the University of California, Berkeley. College would provide the means to the freedom she craved. She received a partial scholarship, took out some loans, and worked in the dormitory and the Student Union cafeteria. Although we had fought all the time when we were little, as normal sisters do, we became extremely close as we got older, so I missed her terribly when she left. I was overwhelmed with emptiness and fear, feeling as if I had been left alone to fend off assaults from an insane world. I knew this was more than a summer away from home: this was my future, living without Sarah nearby.

Sarah, 1949

The affection I had for Sarah in those days was strong but also ensnarled in the weird family roles that had begun in our home. She represented the only sane member of the family, but while I'd spent most of my time at home alone, she had the privilege of a life on the outside. My mother, who functioned normally in daily life and indeed loved me, was, like my father, irreparably damaged emotionally. But once Sarah declared herself non-domestic, she left me holding the bag for all the household responsibilities. Her greater age together with my mother's support seemed to give her more freedom while she still lived at home. I remember being locked in the backyard, watching over the twins and peeking through the screen door behind the house to see her curled up on the floor watching *American Bandstand* or a sci-fi movie. Sarah seemed to me at that time insensitive to my life, not realizing or perhaps not even caring about the tension her insensitivity had created between us. A subtle yet real emotional separation existed, which was maintained throughout our lives, even as adults.

Sarah's perceived freedom, however, did not diminish the effect of my father's vicious treatment of her, especially in high school. As a child she was vehemently opposed to his presence, and I can see this in the photos he took of her. She is often trying to shrink away from the camera. Yet my sister never yielded her independence to my father; a fierce independence was hardwired into her, refusing to bend to his will or to be consumed by his bullying.

Both our parents and Sarah's boyfriend, Mike, and his parents came to Sarah's graduation. My father showed up in one of his manic states, so from the start we knew trouble was brewing. To strangers, he might have appeared overzealous or excitable, but we'd seen this show before and knew how it ended. My father had his ever-present Leica with him and made everyone pose over and over for photo after photo. He told Polish jokes, which no one understood, and at dinner at Spangler's after the ceremony, he dictated to everyone what they should eat. He kept saying about Sarah and me, "They're pretty, but they're stupid. Sarah doesn't even know how to use a knife and fork."

We spent the next day in San Francisco, and Daddy's behavior went from bad to worse. Sarah clung to my mother, begging her to control him, as if she could. Sarah was nervous about what he would do next, and as she later told me, it was one

Bronia and Sarah, 1964, at Berkeley for Sarah's graduation

of the bleakest days of her life—because her fears turned out to be well-founded. Daddy danced in the streets and carried on as a lunatic. I finally got up the courage to say, "Daddy, please don't!"

"Shut up!" he shouted, then reared back and slapped me in the face in front of everyone. Sarah stood by helplessly as this spectacle played out in front of her fiancé and her future in-laws.

Sarah and Mike's wedding, 1964, Los Angeles

Despite my father's antics, Mike was willing to become part of our family. Sarah and Mike were married on August 30, 1964. Their wedding was remarkable, given my parents' lack of funds for a fancy affair. Sarah looked beautiful in a wedding gown straight from Universal Studio's wardrobe department, thanks to Aunt Roselle. It had been made for an actress in *Father of the Bride*, but the gown was too small for her. So Rose Weiss from wardrobe offered it to Sarah, who weighed ninety-two pounds at the time and had to have the gown taken in. We bridesmaids wore bright blue sheath dresses with matching bows for our hair.

Sarah and Nathan, 1947

Many years later, I learned that Sarah was my half sister. Up until then, neither Sarah nor I had any reason to think Mietek Friedland wasn't her father, too. My mother had never told either of us about Nathan.

Sometime in the early 1970s, my childhood friend Bella nonchalantly asked if Sarah had ever met her real father. At first I thought I misunderstood her question, but I soon learned from her that everyone—absolutely everyone we knew except Sarah and me—was aware that Sarah was not Daddy's biological child. I was floored, and immediately called Sarah. Her first reaction was neither anger nor disbelief, but rather pure unadulterated relief that she was not actually related to our violent, unstable father. Sarah called Mom and, without telling her why, announced that she was coming to talk to her. My mother somehow instinctively knew what Sarah wanted to discuss, and waited on the porch for Sarah, holding photos of Nathan.

After that I wondered if perhaps I could extract myself from him as well. I recalled a strange incident from when we lived in City Terrace. The congregation at the Hebrew Folk

School included everyone I knew from the survivor community. At one assembly when I was about six years old, I was listening to the rabbi's sermon about the Holocaust and how lucky we were to reside in Los Angeles. He spoke about a small child who had been orphaned in Europe and found by a Polish couple who took her in as their own. He spoke about how this family immigrated to America and settled in City Terrace. Then he mentioned the adopted child's name—Ruthie Friedland.

I gasped and started to cry when I heard him say my name. The adults at the assembly tried to calm me, telling me the rabbi had made a mistake.

"Of course your parents are Mietek and Bronia, Ruthie. Stop crying. You know who your mommy and daddy are."

"But why would the rabbi talk about me?"

"It was a mistake. It's OK. Calm down."

"I don't understand," I sniffled.

I have never forgotten this experience, and to this day, almost a whole lifetime later, I'm still not 100 percent sure the rabbi was wrong. I'm still haunted by doubt about what the real story might be.

But after thinking it over, no matter how much I wanted to deny it, I came to the conclusion that I must be my father's daughter. I resemble him physically, and like him I've suffered from chronic depression since I was young. My father and I also shared a love of music. When he was hungry and his stomach growled, he'd say, "Chopin is playing in my stomach." I didn't care for his Polish sense of humor, but the Chopin part got to me. I loved learning to play Chopin, and at a young age learned some waltzes and mazurkas, which I've kept in my memory. As time went on, I tried to imagine a world without Chopin, and could not. I have a feeling my father felt the same way. He was speaking metaphorically, distantly, yet sometimes I still find Chopin playing in my soul.

I tried to find Nathan or one of his descendants while working on this book. I had been told he eventually emigrated to Australia and was a chemistry professor. But the accuracy of this information was always in doubt, and I wasn't even sure how to spell his last name. The only objective evidence I have of Nathan's existence is some photos of him with Sarah when she was about three years old. As an adult, Sarah never tried to find her real father. Instead she chose to let the past stay in the past and the skeletons of her life to remain undisturbed. When Sarah's daughter was a student at Berkeley, she chose a study-abroad program in Australia. Sarah and Mike visited her there, and before they departed, Sarah told me she was considering looking up her real father. But she decided against it: "He never bothered to look for me." I had to bite my tongue. The truth was, he had combed the bulletin boards and found her in Berlin to take her and our mother with him. Just as I was about to say this, I stopped myself—believing this was her decision and it would be wrong of me to interfere or even offer my opinion. As a result, disappointingly, I know little about the man who was evidently the love of my mother's life.

This I do know, however. Right before Sarah's wedding, my mother received an envelope in the mail, sent anonymously, containing $3,000. At the time, we believed it must have come from one of our refugee family friends who felt sorry for my mother. Yet recently I have wondered if perhaps Nathan was the source of the mysterious windfall. My mother perhaps had notified him about Sarah's marriage, and I think that despite the twisted history he and my mother shared, Nathan may have still cared deeply about his daughter.

Ruth's high school graduation photo

Chapter 13

HIGH SCHOOL

My mother looked over my report cards when I was a child and praised me for being a good student. But by the time I was in high school, she seemed to have lost interest in anything I did other than helping with household chores. The hierarchy in our family was clear. Sarah was the socially active one, and I was the one who, from second grade until I left the house, took care of my younger siblings, cooked, and cleaned. You might say I was "playing house," as girls often do, except there was no playing involved. When it came time to graduate from Eastmont Junior High in Monterey Park, no one came. Instead, on the same day, I attended my mother's long-awaited graduation ceremonies for her nursing degree.

While my academic performance didn't seem to hold much importance for anyone, I still made good grades—that is, until I encountered statistics and tennis in high school. My statistics teacher was such a bore that I could barely keep my attention on what he was saying. I didn't have trouble with the math, but coming up with an interesting subject for analysis and solving the problem was not easy for me. My teacher said I was not paying attention and would have trouble reading the *Wall Street Journal* when I grew up. He was wrong. I thoroughly enjoy the *Wall Street Journal*, especially the Life & Arts section.

Tennis was above and over my head. I had excellent vision but could never see the ball in time to hit it. The problem must have been hand-eye coordination or lack of strength. I was, however, a fast runner, especially in the fifty-yard dash, and a strong swimmer, and I could play the piano. So I have to conclude that I simply hated playing tennis; it was exhausting and humiliating to chase after every ball, because I couldn't figure out how to get it to make contact with my racket. I failed the class and then took it the next semester, only to fail it again. The curse of tennis almost kept me from graduating. Fortunately, I ended up taking badminton and passed with flying colors.

My first high school was Montebello High, the same school Sarah attended, but my parents decided to move to West LA, thinking I would be in a better school and environment. So only one week after the first term, I enrolled at Alexander Hamilton High School, just a few blocks from where Bella lived. I loved being close to her and her parents; she was in a different grade and classes, but we spent time together in her home. I envied her, being the only child with so many more luxuries than I, and so few responsibilities at home. I was in awe of her powder-blue Geistex sweater, the brand made famous by Natalie Wood. All the girls at our school who were in the "in crowd" and could afford to shop at Jax in Beverly Hills wore these tightly woven sweaters, which also came in bright chartreuse and poison orange. In fact at every high school I attended, brand names were highly important and visible on clothes, shoes, and cars. Even though I was still sewing many of my own clothes, I could not pass the high-fashion test, and imagined that other students could estimate our family income by a quick, once-over glance of what I wore. Bella also had a row of shoes in different styles and colors—flat-heeled pumps in brown or black leather and the popular plain sneakers that came in every shade to match every outfit: white, red, pink, and navy blue. Meanwhile, my standard outfit throughout high school was the same pair of worn-out, black-and-white oxfords with white bobby socks, a pleated plaid skirt with a white shirt, and a red or navy Shetland crewneck cardigan sweater. Despite my love for Bella and her family, like any teenager, I could become consumed with self-pity about being the substantially poorer half of two best girlfriends.

With the dawn of adolescence in my sophomore year, all of a sudden I was interesting to boys—a crisis, as far as my father was concerned. The social structure at Alexander Hamilton High School was much like at college, with clubs mimicking sororities and fraternities. One such club was the Essex, which fielded the male intellectuals who usually landed in Ivy League or other good schools. Though I was surprised—and flattered— when one of them would ask me on a date, since I clearly did not belong to a sorority or wear the right clothes, I happily consented, but I was never asked twice. Where Sarah was smooth and social, I was shy and geeky, and the evenings never went well. Regardless, whenever a boy drove over to pick me up, I had to sneak out of the house, and my mother made sure my father was either asleep or away.

One day Bella said, "Ruthie, you're gaining quite a reputation at school!" I was shocked and crestfallen, mainly because I was too intimidated to kiss and I sure didn't have a clue about how to start making out on these dates. I didn't know how to act around normal teenaged kids. I had no idea where the boundaries were. Bella implied that I had a reputation for being "easy," since the hottest guys were asking me out, but the truth was just the opposite. I was so terrified of my father that I was incapable of being defiant. At the time, I was an innocent and couldn't imagine doing anything as bold as having sex. It was all I could do to carry a conversation, and even then I felt inadequate. The dates ended abruptly, leaving me hopelessly crushed.

I fell hard for one of the boys and desperately wished for him to ask me out again, but it never happened. He soon had a beautiful, socially gracious girlfriend who was a member of a prestigious high school sorority. Ironically, she and I later struck up an acquaintance when she enrolled at UC Berkeley.

At home I told my mother I was worried about what others thought about me. She instinctively understood what I was trying to convey, and said, "Ruthie, just be yourself and you will be all right. Don't listen to what others say." It wasn't much comfort, but the problem was soon solved. Without warning or explanation my family moved again, this time to Van Nuys in

the San Fernando Valley, and I began my third high school—
Birmingham High.

I took all this shuffling in stride, since my parents did what
was necessary to survive without worrying about the adjustments
that lay ahead for their children. I believe my father had lost his
job by this time and my mother got a better job at Valley Presbyterian Hospital. I didn't have one friend at Birmingham High
and would eat lunch alone every day, often in the bathroom. This
school, built just after World War II, had no air-conditioning,
but the girls' bathrooms were large with one wall devoted to a
good-sized mirror and metallic shelf to set books or bags on,
which is what I leaned against while I ignored the surroundings
and ate my lunch. Being in there was better than sitting con-
spicuously alone in a cafeteria where everyone knew each other
and was chatting loudly. I became even more introverted at Birmingham High.

But one day while I was in the cafeteria buying my Jell-O,
a girl next to me casually invited me to a party. Although I didn't
know her well, I decided I would go, mainly out of curiosity. It
was a Friday night, and I arrived at the party alone. I immediately
saw Skip, a tall, good-looking athlete who made my heart flip
every time he glanced my way, so I decided to hang around for a
while. Nearly everyone was smoking and drinking alcohol, and
the room was noisy and crowded. I passed on the drinks, and
soon lost sight of Skip, but after a while, feeling unmoored, I
decided to wander around the house. I walked into an open bedroom and in the light of a small lamp and the moon, I saw Skip,
partially clothed, lying on top of a naked girl. For a moment
I stood frozen and gawking, but then I couldn't get away fast
enough. Outside of what I'd read in books, this was my first
introduction to sex—watching my teenage crush romping in bed
with another girl. This was also the end of my party-going and
my mooning over Skip. I got home early that night, and no one
in the house even noticed I'd been missing.

During one of my solitary lunches, I learned that President Kennedy had been killed. Actually, I had just walked out
of the bathroom and was leisurely walking in the direction of
my next class when I overheard a cluster of kids talking rapidly.
From the tone of their voices I felt something was wrong, so I

stopped to listen. One turned to me and said, "The president was shot and killed." I stammered out the questions, "What? When did this happen? Who did this?" I remember rushing to the classroom where a few students had already arrived and our science teacher was standing in front of the chalkboard. As more students arrived, he asked everyone to put their heads down on their desks, then turned out the lights. We remained still the entire period, and at the end of class he announced that we could go home.

I rushed home, taking the first bus I could find, and saw my mother glued to the TV. Tears were streaming down her face as she looked at me. We hardly said anything to each other but I recall her words: "This is such a tragedy! Ruthie, I don't believe this has happened." My parents seldom discussed politics other than an occasional remark by my father. When Eisenhower was president, my father, in his strange way of being comical, would occasionally shriek, "IKE," followed by loud laughter. In his serious moods, he often said, "Better to be Dead Than Red," and his mouth would always harden. He would mutter, with pronounced sarcasm, "*Pravda*," the Soviet newspaper (which translates as truth).

But during John F. Kennedy's political campaign, my mother vocalized her beliefs clearly. She was enamored by his vitality, his words of statesmanship, and his intellectual breadth, and she feared that his Catholic religion might prevent him from being elected. When Sarah called, we were all numb and grief-stricken. The shock that went through our house persisted—Sarah swore she would never set foot in Texas, and meant it. Twenty-four years later, when I had surgery in Houston, she was torn over the decision to visit me, but reluctantly came. Even while I was recovering, she reminded me that "This was the state where JFK was assassinated."

❧

When one of my classmates at Hamilton High School, the brother of actress Michelle Lee, asked me if I was going on a sophomore field trip to Lake Mammoth, I hoped that being asked to go with him was an invitation to join the in crowd of

Jewish intellectuals. I desperately wanted to be part of their klatch, so I gathered up my nerve, forged my mother's signature on the permission slip, and accompanied the other teens on the trip. We went ski boarding and everything was going fabulously—until I slammed into a tree, smashing my leg. It swelled to twice its size, and my jeans required slicing open to accommodate my bulging limb. Needless to say, I couldn't sneak my gargantuan leg and tattered jeans past my mother. I had to come clean and tell her what I'd done. My mother was calm as we sat and ate our ritual cinnamon toast and drank tea; then she took me to get an X-ray. "Ruthie, you shouldn't have lied about the trip," she said with a world-weary sigh.

"I'm sorry, Mom. I will never do it again. I really, really wanted to go on this trip, and you know how Dad is. He doesn't let me do anything outside the house. It's just not fair."

"I know it is not easy. Believe me, I know your father is difficult. But you should not hide things from me. You have a window in your forehead, and I can always see when you are not being honest. When I was your age, I did almost the same thing, but regretted it. I wanted so much to take part in an ice-skating competition—just as you wanted so much to go on your class trip. But my parents were against my skating that day. I did not understand why they felt as they did. I went on the ice anyway, and while I was skating at the competition, a girl knocked me down and her skate sliced my leg pretty badly. I tried to hide it from my parents, but the infection got so bad I could have lost my leg. The injury was almost in exactly the same place as yours. So now you understand why you should not have tried to hide your injury from me. Look what happens, Ruthie. It is not good, but you're clearly my daughter."

❧

I should have realized that Sarah would still be there for me when she went to university. Late one night, my mother came into my room and woke me up. In a hushed voice, she told me it was too dangerous for me to stay at home anymore—my father's violence had escalated further and she didn't know what he might do to me. She was afraid he would discover that I was going out without his knowledge, and that he might kill me. My mother handed me a cardboard box packed with a few clothes, some cooked chicken, and a ten-dollar bill, and sent me on a Greyhound bus to stay with Sarah in Berkeley. I was devastated. My mother could have fought for me, but instead she shipped me off into the night.

For the next several months I was a lonely vagabond without friends, family, or my beloved piano. Sarah became my legal guardian, which of course added to her responsibilities, including my enrollment in my fourth high school, Berkeley High. I was in a state of shock with everything happening so quickly. One day I was at home, going to high school in Van Nuys, and the next day I was on a bus bound for Berkeley. I was clueless about where to start or what to do.

At Berkeley, a place untarnished by the unhappy family she left behind, Sarah suddenly had me living with her, and I think in her mind I represented the past era of a miserable home life. I could sense her apprehension and felt like an invader. Her studies, jobs, and relationship with Mike kept her so occupied that she had little time for me. I still felt her love, but I was an outsider nonetheless. Not of my own choosing, I was placed in an environment where I could witness firsthand a modern young couple's relationship as they coped with the multiple issues (beyond those due to my living with them) they had to concern themselves with. As I got to know Mike, I inevitably compared him to my father, both Ashkenazi Jews with forceful personalities—intelligent, opinionated, and most certainly of the alpha male type. My complicated emotional relationship with Sarah from that point onward was always one in which Mike played a leading role. I came to understand the depth of their relationship as well as its strengths and weaknesses. And in my own mind I saw how my sister, the person closest to me, interacted with Mike. I saw things I liked and things I didn't like. Of course all of this was reflective and not a point of discussion between Sarah and me. In fact, throughout our lives a barrier seemed to exist that neither she nor I could cross—we could never share the intimacies of our lives as other sisters often do. More sadly, my parents had been instrumental in building this barrier, as they built another to separate their children from themselves.

One day after school, I arrived at our apartment on Roosevelt Street and found a note from the postal service tacked on the door, advising of a package left for us at the post office. I dutifully walked there and signed for the package, thinking it was from my mother. When I got home and opened the box, I was surprised to see it was a bottle of Shalimar perfume. Only then did I look at the box and realize it had Sarah's name on it, not mine.

As I fumbled with the box, the perfume bottle slipped out of my hand and crashed to the floor. Just at that moment, Sarah and Mike walked in and saw me standing in a pool of broken glass with the smell of perfume wafting through the room. Sarah grabbed the box and screamed at me, "Ruthie, you broke my bottle of *Shalimar*! It was a gift from Mike's mother. How did you get it?" I explained about going to the post office, thinking it was a gift from Mom, and signing for it without looking at the return address. At this point, Mike led Sarah out the front door for a private conversation, and while I was trying to clean up, they came back in. Mike shouted at me, pointing his forefinger in my face, "Do you know you committed fraud? Do you know you can be arrested for this crime?"

I just stood there in disbelief, shaking from horror and embarrassment. I was a criminal! In my head, I kept hearing over and over again, "*Shalimar,* Sarah's favorite perfume and a gift from Mike's mother!" Mike and Sarah left the apartment, and I spent a miserable, guilty evening at home alone.

I felt as if I was a burden, and looking back, I'm sure I was. Sarah taught me how to find books in the stacks of the impressive Berkeley library, but she and her fiancé and their friends sat at their own table. I felt lonely at the huge college, but also sophisticated—a high school student roaming the beautiful Berkeley campus. Although it was a relief to be away from my father's unpredictable explosions, Sarah couldn't be expected to take the place of parents for a lonesome teenager. I missed my mother, but understood why she had sent me away—at least on an intellectual level. On an emotional level, I felt abandoned.

For some reason I never panicked, assuming everything would fall into place. The truth was, I desperately needed guidance and a calm environment. But I was in for a pleasant surprise: quietly drifting around my new environs, I met a couple of girls at school, Lisa and Toni, who became my friends and helped fill out the weekends. Lisa had just moved from Chapel Hill, North Carolina, to Berkeley, where her father, a sociology professor, had taken a position on the UC faculty. Toni had just returned home from a private school in Switzerland, where her parents thought she would benefit from not only the academics, but also the culture and languages. Toni's father was a chemistry professor, her mother, a German language professor at UC. Her mother often invited me to their home on weekends for teatime. They lived in a Spanish stucco house on Grizzly Peak with a view of the entire San Francisco Bay, including all the bridges. The garden was terraced and lush with crimson begonias and periwinkle, and petunias bordered the lawn in a profusion of bright colors. Brilliant fuchsias hung against the exterior walls of the house. Leafy trees provided shade for a linen-covered table where we ate strawberries and little cakes. This did not look or feel anything close to the City Terrace crowd's teatime, and I was wide-eyed with the splendor of the scene.

On many Sundays, Toni's father would take us to his favorite museum, The Palace of the Legion of Honor, which was a gift from the heirs of the Spreckels Sugar family and which overlooks the Golden Gate Bridge. The three of us would walk through the galleries of Rodin sculptures; versions of his most famous works *The Thinker* and *The Kiss* are among this collection. We also surveyed the collection of Impressionist and European paintings, as well as ancient and decorative arts. It was the first time I'd stood in front of a Rembrandt, El Greco, Renoir, Degas, or Monet, and I was mesmerized. The grand finale, Toni laughingly told me, had become *raison d'etre* for the outings for her father. We would all head to the little café downstairs where we enjoyed pie or cake and coffee while he jokingly flirted with the waitresses. My world had changed so drastically that I blocked out the troubles at home, and also felt I was forgotten there.

Nonetheless, this arrangement was particularly onerous for Sarah. She wanted to spend every spare minute with her boyfriend, Mike, although she was still living with her roommate Marcia at the time. Of course I was in the way—a high school student doesn't fit in at a college apartment. Sarah was busy studying, working, or socializing, and being with her future husband, Mike. Most of the time I ate alone because they were dining in the Student Union cafeteria, where they both worked. On weekends we shopped at the Co-op (now Whole Foods, originally an Austin company) and bought bargain foods for the apartment. Marcia, who was from a wealthy family, stocked the cupboards with luxury items such as canned cherries in syrup, which of course were for her use only. But I sometimes transgressed and could not resist the temptation of those cherries. I even ate a whole can on one occasion, knowing I would incur the wrath of Marcia.

Since I spent much time after school alone, my salvation was a high school drama class, where I was first exposed to the genre of dramatic literature. One of the plays we studied was *The Glass Menagerie*, by Tennessee Williams, and the teacher chose me to play the part of Laura. I was thrilled, and threw myself into studying my lines and learning the part's characteristic limp. Laura, a complex, sad character, is dominated by her mother, Amanda, and it occurred to me that there were parallels in our lives. Laura's mother lives in the past, a time when she was young and sought after by men. After her husband abandons her, she and her children have to eke by socially and financially. She burdens Laura with lofty expectations to replace her losses—much like my father, who had the same obsessions and hardships, but for different reasons. Both Amanda's and my father's psychological frailties had a profound effect on their daughters: Laura is a misfit, misunderstood, and a shy and socially awkward girl who depends on her glass animals as much as I depended on my music and piano to survive in a dysfunctional family.

⟿

The irony of fleeing my chaotic and dangerous household in 1964 to go to Berkeley, the epicenter of the Free Speech Movement

(FSM), was lost on me at the time. But in retrospect, Berkeley, even with the campus sit-ins and demonstrations, seemed calm to me compared to living with my father. Being a sixteen-year-old in Berkeley, with only Sarah—who had little patience for me—for guidance, left me feeling disoriented. I tried to comprehend the sit-ins and mass demonstrations of the FSM. Names like Jerry Rubin, Angela Davis, Betina Aptheker, and others floated around. Later, as a student at San Francisco State from 1968 to 1969, I was in the midst of a landmark student-led strike, the longest campus strike in United States history, its implications extending even until today with relevance to equality and social justice. For five months I watched and read, along with the rest of America, as National Guard troops were called in to form a line across campus that students who were not striking had to break through to get to classes. My beloved classes like Molière to Ibsen were canceled! The linguist S.I. Hayakawa was president of that campus at the time.

In 1968 a coalition of various student groups on college campuses across California responded to the perceived Eurocentric education and lack of diversity at their respective universities, most notably at San Francisco State College and the University of California, Berkeley. The activists were instrumental in creating and establishing Ethnic Studies and other identity studies as majors in their respective schools and universities across the United States. Sarah and I strongly agreed with the attitudes, but perhaps not the aggressive, sometimes bullying methods of the activists. Because of our family background and history, we were often put off by the dogmatic, potentially violent behavior of some more extreme elements of the movement.

꒰ ꒱

After Sarah was married, I went back to LA for the summer. By then I was a seventeen-year-old girl with no money, and without Sarah, had no place to live in Berkeley. But before I even left, I knew I wanted to return to Berkeley High School in the fall to graduate. I was through living in my father's house and being a target for his rages and beatings. Fortunately, I answered an ad pinned to the bulletin board at the university Student Union seeking a college student who could work for room and board. The woman who placed the ad, Annabelle, was the first woman to graduate from the Berkeley School of Architecture. She owned a large home on the beautiful north side of campus, a hilly spread with groves of trees lining The Alameda boulevard. Annabelle rented out four rooms to college students and wanted another student to cook and clean for the boarders. I was doing well at my interview—until I began to collapse under the pressure of being a high schooler trying to pass myself off as a college student. Suddenly I burst into tears and blurted out the truth. As it turned out, Annabelle was sympathetic about my predicament and gave me the job anyway.

My mother came to visit me in the fall, and after I gave her a tour of the house, she began to cry. She felt ashamed that her daughter was working as a maid; it didn't dawn on her that I was doing the same things I had done at home every day. The difference was, at Annabelle's I could work without my father's thrashings and threats, so it was a much better deal for me. I was allowed to borrow Annabelle's daughter's bicycle to travel back and forth to school. Her daughter was away at Antioch College, and when she came home for holidays, I served her as well. But I had more freedom in Berkeley than I'd ever had at home.

I graduated from Berkeley High School in January 1965, a semester early. Since no one was around to attend my high school graduation ceremony, I skipped it, too. Basically, I had more important things to worry about than graduating from high school, because a month later I was going to be married.

Chapter 14

OATHS AND VOWS

A young bride at home, 1968

Growing up with my father could have been enough to keep me away from men for several lifetimes. But curiously, despite all the screaming, violence, and sheer lunacy, my father did not scare me away from them. I fell in love and was married the day after my eighteenth birthday.

When I was home from Berkeley for Sarah's wedding, in the summer of 1964, my friend Suzy wanted to fix me up with her boyfriend's friend, Ron. But he couldn't call me, since my father kept a lock on the house phone so that no one else could use it. So he came by our house to check me out. I was cleaning the bathtub when the doorbell rang, and answered the door wearing a red-and-white-checkered sleeveless shirt, red capri pants, and those ever-fashionable yellow rubber gloves. This was how I met my future husband. He was nice looking and drove a baby-blue MGB convertible, and I was smitten. Of course, I had to see him out of the house, with only my mother knowing where I was going, while my father slept or was at work.

Ron was quick and intelligent, had a great sense of humor, and could always make me laugh. We dated for the rest of the summer until I returned to Berkeley to finish high school and he remained in LA for his sophomore year of college. An English major, he had a talent for writing and wrote to me every day.

Once, he took me to a nightclub to hear the great jazz pianist Les McCann, and my mother, appreciating my thrill about going someplace sophisticated, gave me money to buy a new dress. I picked out a red-and-black Swiss polka dot, scoop-neck sheath dress that I thought made me look more grown-up. We sat at a table near the piano, and I could feel Ron's excitement. Seated on the piano bench, Les McCann turned to face me, gave me a big smile, and asked in a humorous but soft husky voice, "Are you fifteen?" So much for looking sophisticated—but I didn't care, I just laughed.

Other times, we went to the record store on Hollywood Boulevard that had private booths where you could listen to recordings without having to buy them. We would go back and forth into each other's booths, listening to each other's music. I hated the evenings to end.

Or we went to a Jewish deli on Ventura Boulevard called King Solomon's, where for the first time I enjoyed bagels with lox and cream cheese, black Greek olives, and even cream soda. We saw foreign or other popular films such as *La Belle de Nuit*, *The Bicycle Thief*, *The 400 Blows*, and *The Umbrellas of Cherbourg*. On weekends when he wasn't working, we sometimes drove to Solvang, a touristy Danish village where we wandered around the bakeries and bought delicious cheese bread. The hour-and-a-half ride was dreamy. Being loved by Ron was unlike anything I had experienced before. He was gentle and gave so much of himself, without demands of servitude or strict rules—the opposite of my father. We never really argued and seldom was there any tension between us.

Soon my mother became fond of Ron and persuaded my father to allow me to have a boyfriend. He was allowed in to pick me up and bring me home, and it didn't take him long to learn the dysfunctional dynamics of my family life. In my mother he saw her sweet disposition, kindness, selflessness, generosity, and a pervasive sadness, and he thought part of her charm and warmth came from her adorable Polish accent. Many people who knew her felt the same. When we came home late and she would be returning from work, we'd sit at the dining table drinking tea or coffee, eating cinnamon toast, and talking.

She would stress the importance of education above possessions, because she saw in her life how quickly material things could vanish. She spoke of her disappointment in people at work who she felt lacked standards. Her life had been so unpredictable, chaotic, and unfair that she naturally gravitated toward intangibles: ethics, morals, and education. These were attributes no one could take away from her.

My mother's social life seemed terribly limited. In the early 1950s, my father had accused her of trying to poison him, and as a result, forbade her to buy groceries. She never again went to the store, but would send me to pick up whatever she needed for herself. I had a perennial signed note requesting cigarettes from the checkout clerk at the nearest market or drugstore. Her friends were more acquaintances and were limited to the nurses and people she worked with. Or occasionally she would briefly chat with a neighbor passing by. These people seldom if ever came into our home. By now, the Jacksons and Kingstons lived far from us and rarely visited.

When at home and not sleeping, she was often sullen and tired. Her face became more and more strained. But whenever Ron visited our house, which he did regularly in the summer, she came back to life. He managed to cheer her up even when she was down, especially after she came home from work. One night, in his tone-deaf, faux-operatic baritone, he croaked *Carmen* to my mother in Polish:

Powiedz mi, Carmen, jeśli kochasz mnie,
ja kocham cię, ale ty nie kochasz mnie też.

He managed the first line pretty well, he thought, until Mom laughed and pleaded with him to stop. She said, "You are telling me, '*Carmen, go hang yourself.*'"

Her laughter was contagious and it warmed my heart to hear it. Sadly, she had managed to escape the horrors of a political system bent on her destruction only to find a domestic "refuge" of house arrest, impoverishment, and abuse. Jews know themselves as "God's chosen people," a phrase generating much enmity from people of other religions for many centuries. In Judaism, though, rather than signifying entitlement, "chosen" means selected by God to be tested in our faith. I think my mother aced her test.

She told Ron about Jim Krebs of the LA Lakers who was killed in a freak accident when a tree fell on him. She was on duty at Valley Presbyterian Hospital when they brought him into the emergency room. "Poor man," she said. "No one should die like this." Her words gave Ron a lump in his throat as he pondered the enormity of the human suffering she had seen and endured in her lifetime.

Typically, Ron came to our apartment after his work shift at the A&P grocery, still wearing his checker uniform—black slacks, white shirt, and black tie. On one occasion, my father sat him at the dining table with a plate of tripe, which he had cooked himself, and in his heavy Polish accent, asked, "Ron, how much did this tie cost you?" Ron, trying to keep a straight face, both from having the *r* in his name trilled at length and from guessing the direction this conversation was going, answered, "I'm not sure, Mr. Friedland, but I think it was ninety-nine cents plus tax."

My father replied, again with a long trill of the *r*, "Ron, when I was your age, I would go to London, Savile Row—you know what Savile Row is?"

"Yes, fine clothes."

"When I came in, they would say, 'Ah, Mr. Friedland from Warsaw, how are you? May we show you something today?' 'Yes, I want to see silk ties.' They would show me ties, the very latest, most expensive, and I would pick the finest. 'May we show you anything else, Mr. Friedland?' 'Yes, I'd like some suits to match the ties!'" he said, and laughed loudly. "See, when *you* buy a suit, Ron, you get a tie to match it. When *I* bought a tie, I got suits to match it!"

Suddenly, my father howled, "I was the *Prince of Poland!*"

He paused, obviously shaken, then gruffly added, "Eat your tripe."

⁓

In January 1965, my mother realized I was finishing school and saw a bleak future stretched out before her. It was becoming increasingly difficult for her to manage the twins, her work, and my father by herself. She announced, "Ruthie, you cannot go back to Berkeley. I need you at home! You must live here again, because I need your help."

"Mom, I can't. I just can't. I want to go to college in Northern California. Ron is planning to transfer to San Francisco State so we can be together."

My mother persisted. "No, I need you here. You have to stay at home. I can't do it without you."

I pleaded with her. "I can't go back to the way my life was when I lived here all the time. Can't you understand what it was like for me?"

She continued to argue and finally was reduced to threats as I continued to object. "This is what is going to happen. You are coming back home to live, and you can go to college here in Los Angeles. This is the way it's going to turn out."

"No, I won't do it," I said firmly.

"If you won't do as I say, I'll disown you and not support your education."

I laughed when she said this, because if she had stopped to think, she would have realized she hadn't supported me while I was in high school either. I knew returning home meant I would once again become the household slave and be victimized by my father. The twins were eleven years old then, and they were a handful.

I was in a terrible situation; I loved my mother, but I'd had enough of indentured servitude, especially after having experienced the freedom of being on my own. Ron and I were sure of us as a couple, and our love and commitment to each other was so strong it required no formal proposal. We knew for certain we would eventually marry. With this new crisis at hand, we mutually decided to get married in February, to live and work in Los Angeles until the following semester, and then move back to Berkeley. We were aware of the serious commitment of marriage, but after living apart and missing each other so much, we felt ready to take the big leap, despite our young ages. My mother's demand for me to once again be the vassal of her household spurred our decision to get married right away.

❧

Ron's mother didn't like me. It probably wasn't actually me she had qualms about, but rather the *idea* of me.

When I first started dating Ron, he had just broken up with Barbara, who was from a wealthy family. His parents lived in Van Nuys then, but were originally East Coast Jews. Ron's mother never met Barbara's parents because he refused to subject them to her "unique" personality. She considered them snobbish rich people who looked down on her. So when I came along, she welcomed the opportunity to flip the situation and look down on someone else. Ron's mother saw me as a tremendous comedown for her son. She was so opposed to the idea of us getting married she announced that she wouldn't attend our wedding. Not only did she forbid him to marry, she even packed all his belongings in boxes and attached a note, saying, "Get out!" No chance for misinterpretation there. Ron had been living on his own since he was eighteen, and had moved back home only to save money for college, which he financed himself by working as a grocery clerk. He brushed off the eviction as one of his mother's hysterical reactions to people who refused to bend to her will.

My mother, always seeing the best in people, decided the three of us (my father was left out for obvious reasons) should go visit his parents and persuade them to come to the wedding. Despite Ron's warning that such a meeting would be painful and pointless, a week before the wedding we traipsed over to their house.

As we sat on a plastic-covered faux–French Provincial couch, my mother calmly and sweetly said to Ron's parents, "We would very much like you to come to the wedding. It will be a small affair, but I know Ron and Ruthie want you to attend. It would mean a lot to them, and to my husband and me, if you would come."

My mother had little opportunity to continue since Ron's mother interrupted her to say what a horrible situation I had thrown their family into. Both of Ron's parents became more and more agitated, their voices grew louder, and it became clear that she looked down on my family because we were refugees. She asked, "What kind of a parent would allow her daughter to live alone in Berkeley, a haven for liberals and communists?"

The conversation did not go well. My mother remained quiet and dignified as she listened to Ron's mother heap criticism on us. Only after Ron's mother implied I was a slut who had corrupted and muddled her precious son's thinking with premarital sex, did my mother stand up to leave. She softly said, "I faced Hitler and the Nazis, but I never met people like this." And she walked out, her back straight, her head held regally.

After my mother left, Ron, who was not surprised by his mother's neurotic behavior but disappointed in his father's lack of courage, looked at his parents in disgust and said, "By the way, Dad, who does your thinking for you?" The three of us squeezed back into the baby-blue MGB, and drove away. When we got home, we sat around the kitchen table having my mother's panacea: tea and cinnamon toast. I think my mother felt sorry for Ron upon discovering what kind of parents he had.

The day before my wedding, my parents broke tradition by joining forces to give me a beating I would never forget—as if my father's singular beatings weren't severe enough. I had spent time with my future husband the day before the wedding, contrary to their strongly held superstitions, and they were scandalized. They screamed at me that it was unlucky to spend time with your intended before taking your vows. My father whaled me with his belt, and my mother punched and slapped me. My mother's fury surprised me, but she had a temper, too—it was just usually eclipsed by my father's. This time, however, I had deliberately violated one of her sacred superstitions, and her anger got the best of her.

Their superstition turned out as imagined, a self-fulfilling prophecy, since the purple welts all over my body proved how unlucky breaking this tradition could be. When Sarah came home for my wedding, she found me bruised and beaten, crying in a heap in a corner of the bedroom we used to share. She dropped her luggage and immediately put her arms around me, holding me gently. I could hardly move, could hardly get the words out to explain what had happened, but I could feel her love and empathy toward me. It was all a blur of pain and emotions, of hatred toward my parents, and disbelief of how they treated me. I was sobbing, but Sarah instinctively understood. She was appalled by how vicious my parents had been, and comforted me by saying, "After today, you will never have to deal with this again."

On my wedding day, February 21, 1965, as I was getting into the car in my eleven-dollar on-sale wedding dress, my father noticed I had a little makeup on. "You whore!" he shrieked, and struck me so hard across the face he almost knocked me out. What had begun for me as the most thrilling weekend of my life turned into one more inexplicable nightmare—except I did get married to a man I loved.

The wedding was a small event—about twenty-five people in a little chapel. After the ceremony, my parents had a reception at their house with the usual delicatessen staples: corned beef, pastrami, and lox. My father bought the food, and the neighbors helped set it out.

Ron and I didn't have much of a honeymoon. We were married on President's Day, and the next day was a regular school and work day. The morning after my wedding, my father, smartly dressed in a suit and hat, unexpectedly showed up at our newlywed apartment. Although I was still angry with him, I was respectful. I would never slam the door in his face, so I invited him into the apartment. Before I could offer him some coffee, he went directly into the bedroom and looked around. What was he doing, checking the sheets? I didn't say anything to him because it was so typical of my father's Old World attitudes, and so representative of our relationship—which was, to put it delicately, complicated. He stayed with me the whole day. When Ron came home from work, the three of us went to see the Russian film version of the opera *Eugene Onegin*. With its themes of miscommunications, jealousy, star-crossed timing, and unrequited love, this Pushkin tale was the frosting on the cake of what had to be one of the worst and shortest honeymoons on record.

Bronia in her nurse's uniform, Los Angeles, 1951

Chapter 15

THE GREAT ESCAPE

L ater that year, my mother finally had enough. I don't know
how she had weathered all my father's highs and lows up to
then. Everyone's breaking point is different, and my mother put
up with an awful lot in the twenty-plus years she was with him.
I now recognize that she was in a no-win situation for many of
those years. How could she run away from Daddy with four
children in tow, no one to help her, and no place to go? She really
had no choice.

The straw that finally broke the back of their relationship
seems rather mundane in the context of my father's many diabol-
ical diatribes; but, as of a glass filled to the brim, the next drop
was just too much.

My parents had been expecting houseguests, so Daddy
went out to shop in anticipation of the company. While he was
out, the houseguests came and went. When he returned, my
father was furious that they had already left, and accused my
mother of not entertaining them properly. He grabbed a glass
bottle of 7UP from his grocery bag and hurled it across the room.
Green glass and sticky liquid exploded in front of her. Apparently this was all it took for my mother to finally realize she'd had

too much of Daddy. She knew in her bones it was time to leave. After so many years of acquiescing to his abuse, Mom had one last ion of bravery left in her, and it was ignited by the shards of a green soda bottle.

Newly married Ron and I, Sarah and Mike, all of us were living in Berkeley. My mother phoned and told me she had to get out right away. I arranged to fly to Los Angeles with Ron, and met her at the airport to assist in her escape. Mom took only things that were really important to her—the twins, her naturalization papers, her nursing license—and nothing else. She packed no clothing for herself or the twins, and no household items. She was afraid to take anything else with her, because she didn't want to arouse my father's suspicion until she was long gone.

When I looked for my mother at our designated meeting place in the airport, I didn't see her. Then I heard a whisper.

"Ruthie, here I am." She was hiding behind a large rubber tree plant. She held each of the twins close to her side.

"What are you doing there, Mom?"

"I'm so afraid he will find me."

I was struck for the first time by how frightened she was of my father and his skills at revenge and cruelty. She had always tried to mask her feelings, but when I saw her ducking behind the plant, I knew she was far more terrified than she had ever let on. We all flew back to Berkeley together.

Soon my mother found a job at Alta Bates Hospital. Sarah and I found her an apartment close by and enrolled the twins in school. Except for work, my mother was too petrified to go out of the apartment. I would check on her every morning, and every day she would cautiously look out the peephole before opening the door for me. Surrounded by dull gray walls, the living room of this dinky apartment was sparsely furnished with a small vinyl sofa, a chair, and a small table. The only color in the room was provided by the twins, propped up on the little sofa, looking bewildered and sad. The twins' lives had been suddenly upended, and they were miserable. Freddy was in tears since arriving at the airport, realizing he would not be able to play baseball with his Little League team. He was a naturally gifted baseball player, and for the first time was getting attention from his peers and having some real fun in his life. He was devastated by this sudden move and refused to speak a word for the first six months after they left Los Angeles. Fortunately, his science teacher, Mr. Williams, took an interest in this quiet, melancholy boy and helped him recuperate from his emotional trauma.

My brother, Fred

My mother flitted around in a constant state of fear and depression. She had no car and nothing to set up an apartment. Sarah and I gave her dishes, pots and pans, towels, and linens from our wedding presents, but once again, my poor mother was a refugee, forced to start from scratch.

My father soon figured out that my mother must have gone to Berkeley. He called constantly, but we wouldn't give him any information—it was only a matter of time before he showed up. One day I came home from work and found a stack of steaks on my front porch. I didn't have to think for a minute—I immediately knew my father, bearing steaks from the meatpacking plant, was close by. It gave me the creeps. Sarah and Mike discovered a similar pile of steaks at their apartment door.

Unnerved by what he might do to my mother, we called nearby hotels until we found where Daddy was staying. Mike called his brother-in-law, Larry, who was a psychiatrist in Los Angeles and who told us to contact the police, have my father arrested, and have a restraining order filed against him, which is what happened. He spent the night in jail and then was flown back to LA where Larry had him hospitalized. Turning my father in was traumatic and heartrending, but Sarah and I couldn't conceive of any other option. Our mother's safety was too important, and we all knew the outcome if he ever found her.

To have him committed to the psychiatric hospital in LA, my mother had to file a "Mental Illness Petition." Sarah, or possibly a social worker, helped her write it and my mother signed it. I still have the petition, dated June 24, 1966, which reads in part as follows:

> *From the time I first knew him, I have been aware of his uncontrollable temper, but his personality has grown progressively worse over the years. He has always been extremely demanding and thoughtless of others to the extent that his family were in need while he spent his earnings on himself. It has never been possible to reason with him, as this would cause him to show even more loss of self-control. During his outbursts, he would be destructive and would strike members of the family with his fists and objects, causing injury. He has always been suspicious of others, accusing people of plotting against him and his conduct has estranged those who have tried to be friendly toward him. He intimidates the family by making threats of suicide and, on one occasion that I can recall, four years ago, he tried to suffocate himself by placing a plastic bag over his head. He was hospitalized on an emergency basis, but released in care of his brother with a plan to seek psychiatric treatment. However, this plan never developed. I feel my husband has become progressively worse, but was not aware of how to seek help for him. He is now suspicious to the degree that he believes people are spying on him and he accuses me of trying to poison him. For this reason, he has thrown out food I have bought, making his own purchases. . . . Because of my foreign background, I have always accepted my husband's behavior, but now feel he is a definite danger to the lives of his family and himself. I left home on June 19, 1966, taking our eleven-year-old twins with me, after a violent outburst on the*

part of my husband. . . . In the presence of our children, he used filthy and vulgar language, which he shouted loudly and struck me. I have never considered separation from my husband, and I do not feel his behavior is caused by domestic friction, but rather feel he is mentally ill and in need of hospital care, which he has refused to consider.

We waited for word of my father, praying they wouldn't let him out, since we were all panicked about what he might do. He stayed in the hospital for quite a while but was eventually released in the custody of Josef. He knew that if he tried to see my mother again, he would be arrested. It was nine years before I saw Daddy again. I was scared to go near him.

And the steaks went directly into the garbage.

Curt, Mom, Sarah, and her two daughters, in Ukiah, CA

Chapter 16

IN THE YEARS THAT FOLLOWED

After my mother left my father, she continued to work as a registered nurse and eventually met Curt Sebeck, a cancer patient at Alta Bates Hospital in Berkeley. Curt was immediately attracted to my mother, calling her "Blondie" while she cared for him and visiting her in the hospital even after his release. He was the polar opposite of my father—good-natured, soft-spoken, gentle, and strong. Curt was also quite handsome—tall, blue-eyed, with a full head of beautiful white hair.

They married in 1970, the same year my parents divorced, and remained together until his death in 1992 at the age of ninety-six. Curt was much older than my mother, and he treated her exactly as she deserved. The new marriage meant additional moves for her and the twins—first to Santa Rosa, then to Clearlake, and finally to Ukiah in Mendocino County. Although these were satisfying years for my mother, they were ones of upheaval and uncertainty for the twins. Curt was loving and caring, and made every effort to act as a father, but his relationship with the twins came at a time when they were finally settling in to their new lives in Berkeley. Suddenly they were taken away again to different towns and new schools. The multiple moves in their early years of adolescence left them feeling alienated, and created emotional, scholastic, and physical hardships. Between the ages of eleven and seventeen, their lives were regularly disrupted, and the insecurities inherent in shifting between vastly different communities were tacked on to previous years of living with a mentally unstable father. At school they struggled to make friends, adjust to new social norms, and study effectively. My mother had little time to devote to them as she held a full-time job and spent her free hours with her new husband. Santa Rosa, Clearlake, and especially Ukiah, where they spent most of their remaining youths, were a far cry from either Los Angeles or the vibrant, invigorating college town of Berkeley.

When Gazelle was eighteen, she and my mother decided it would be advantageous for her to live close to me in San Mateo. She arrived sullen, scared, and pencil-thin, having lost a great deal of weight since I last saw her. Ron arranged for her to receive her high school equivalency degree, taught her how to drive, and cosigned a loan on a new car for her. She lived with us, sleeping on the sofa of our one-bedroom apartment. The company I worked for hired her as a rental agent, and before long she had an apartment within a stone's throw from ours. I saw her every day in the next few years—she blossomed in the San Francisco-area environment, making new friends, wearing stylish new clothes, and sporting a fashionable haircut. Gazelle was transformed into a breathtakingly beautiful, tall girl with snow-white skin and gorgeous eyes. Wherever we went, heads turned to stare at her.

Fred was on his own for a while, eventually landing in a hospital for drug abuse. Once home again, my mother convinced him to join Job Corps. She had seen an advertisement for this job-training agency that helped people enter the work force, and pleaded with him to give it a try. He performed so well on the Job Corps entrance examinations that he received a full scholarship to attend Westminster College in Salt Lake City, where he graduated four years later with a bachelor's degree and a major in psychology. He moved back to the Bay Area and lived and worked in Oakland, first in the Probation Department of Human Services and then in various homes for incorrigible boys. He later changed his career and went into sales.

Gazelle at a party in the San Francisco Bay Area, 1975

My mother loved Ukiah. Its bucolic setting amidst verdant landscape brought back fond memories of her quaint, pretty hometown in Poland. It had a small population and was mostly agricultural, famous for its pear orchards and the almonds it produced and exported.

The home Curt had built many years before was surrounded by small cottages that he leased to people in the community. As a result, neighbors lived close by, but the landscape provided enough distance for privacy. The various fruit trees—apricot, apple, plum, and pear—added ample shade and gave even more beauty to the shared property. My mother's dream of coming to America, where she could reach up and pick fruit from the trees, was finally a reality.

When she retired from Ukiah Valley Medical Center, she continued as a volunteer at the same hospital until she died. The troubling aspect of Ukiah, where everyone knew each other's business, was the anti-Semitism that was unfortunately alive and flourishing. When Curt returned to live in Ukiah with his new bride, their neighbors noticed her foreign accent and soon unleashed a distaste for Jews. My mother attempted to obtain her driver's license the maximum number of times allowed, but was refused each time. She always did fine on the tests and was convinced that the only explanation for being denied a license was her Jewishness and her obvious Eastern Bloc origins.

Some of the people in Ukiah were bold enough to comment out loud about my mother's heritage, which was quite different from theirs. At her bedside when she lay dying, I heard one of the nurses say, "She's the Jewish immigrant from Europe." It broke my heart to hear this, since she had dedicated more than twenty years of her life to this very hospital. Her ambition was to help people in need. Of course, not everyone she knew was close-minded and many people loved her, but it was most certainly a painful reminder of all that she had endured earlier in life.

My mother had a massive stroke on November 6, 1996, and spent the next two days alone on her kitchen floor until the gardener discovered her. She died on November 11 (exactly four years after Curt's death) at age seventy-nine. The circumstances of her death still haunt me. I visualize her deteriorating state, lying on the floor, alone and helpless. Mentally, I find myself going over every facet of her last days.

I know she voted the day before her stroke, because the details of her voting choices lay on the kitchen table. Ever since she'd become a US citizen, she never failed to vote and would always prepare by reading as much as she could beforehand. She and Curt always joked about the fact he was Republican and she a Democrat, but he could never change her political views. Next to the ballot information on her kitchen table were cards and notes from her patients expressing gratitude for her help and for the carnations she often took to their sickbeds. Also resting on the table was an invitation from a former gentleman patient who lived alone and wanted to take her out to lunch.

Only a short time before her stroke, Sarah and Mike had found a new home in El Cerrito with perfect quarters for my mother, so she could be close to family. She agreed to this new living arrangement, even though up until then she had preferred to live alone in Ukiah. Unfortunately, their plans came too late.

In spite of the mean-spiritedness of some in Ukiah, dozens of people turned out for my mother's funeral service. They were mostly ordinary people—neighbors who remembered this petite, nicely dressed woman with a friendly smile on her morning walks. Although the director of the hospital attended the service, I was surprised to see only a few of my mother's colleagues from the hospital.

In the early 1970s, the Kingstons' son, Abbe, was getting married and they invited me to the wedding. They also invited my father. I felt conflicted when I saw him, still fearing and hating him because of how he acted during my youth. But in some profound way it was good to see him after all those years apart. He didn't seem to have aged, and he looked healthy, dignified, and more reserved. He was meticulously dressed for this formal occasion, and as I looked at him, I could tell he was less than comfortable about seeing me again. Behind his joy of our reunion, however, was his love for my mother. I knew this and felt it intensely.

The wedding was a grand affair with an orchestra playing during dinner. My father approached me to ask me to dance, and I barely took a step before he hugged and kissed me, telling me how much he missed me. With heaviness in my heart, I continued to let him hold me, then he asked the question he would be repeating every time I saw him after that: "How's Mommy?" He never stopped asking about my mother, and, I think, never stopped loving her.

I gradually started visiting him again in Los Angeles, often asking my childhood friend Bella to accompany me as a buffer. An invaluable ally, she readily agreed to come with me whenever I asked. My father eventually accepted that my mother was not coming back, and at age fifty-nine, started dating again. In 1976, he married Regina, also a Polish refugee, and stayed with her until his death in 1994, despite their tumultuous relationship.

Finally I was able to see my father as a pathetic soul. He was tormented by mental illness and deafness most of his life, but he had moments when he could be charming and generous. When he was eighty-two, he attended my second wedding, gave me a big check, and apologized for the way he had treated me as a child. He said, "This is to make up for all the dinners you cooked and car payments you made for me." Although I could not possibly erase all the bad memories of my youth, his attempt to correct his failures of the past and acknowledge that he treated me so poorly meant a lot. I was touched by the way he presented this gift, but also surprised by his remarks. His words of contrition told me he was not totally insane. If he were, he would not have been able to recall or feel the need to repay me for damages. I never felt the need to forgive him, because I came to understand that it was never his intent to mistreat and abuse us or to neglect his responsibilities as a father. He was not in control of his actions, and as a father and husband he was miserable, without knowing how to prevent himself from being so. He grieved unbearable losses, was tortured, and suffered emotional anguish from 1939 until the day he died.

On January 17, 1994, at 4:31 a.m. PST, the Northridge earthquake struck, killing an estimated sixty people and injuring more than 8,700. The earthquake was so violent it was felt as far away as Las Vegas, and it caused an estimated $20 billion in damages, making it one of the most costly natural disasters in US history. The Los Angeles neighborhood struck the hardest was near my father's apartment. His neighborhood was decimated, and his apartment building in Sherman Oaks was one of the only buildings left standing on his block.

The destruction set something off in my father's mind—he went into a deep depression and was hospitalized in June. He kept saying: "It's just like the war. Everything is broken." He suffered a mild stroke while in the hospital and was eventually transferred to a convalescent home. I was at the piano playing the Schumann composition *Kreisleriana* when I received a phone call from his doctor saying the end was near, and I can never hear this piece without thinking about my father's death. I visited him at the rest home and found my usually impeccably dressed father in a wheelchair, dressed in cheap pants and a polyester shirt, with his arms in restraints. He had lost so much weight he was just skin over bones, and his pallor and jaundice told me his body was starting to shut down. Seeing my father this way tore my heart open. I knew of his violent temper and the reason for the restraints, but watching him struggle to survive and be free made me realize what the doctors did not know about him. He was mentally back in the Russian prison, yet was lucid enough to understand that he was going to die. This time, however, he had neither the strength nor energy to fight back against the constraints and torture.

My father pointed to the sky and told me, "That's where I'm going." It was clear the end was only a hair's breadth away and his lifetime of suffering would soon be over. Two days later, on August 17, 1994, he died. Strangely, I grieved for him far more than for my mother. Given all he put me through in my early life, I still had a great deal of pity for him and was able somehow to connect with him—to appreciate his neediness, his failures, and his inability to turn back time and make things right.

⌒

Fred now works as a real estate agent in the Bay Area. Through his hobby of ice-skating, he made some friends who were Buddhists, and was impressed with how they worked through their difficulties by turning frustrations into something positive. He had been an agnostic for most of his life because he could not accept the Supreme Being concept, but he became more open to spirituality and found great comfort in his new faith.

Fred continued to find solace in Buddhism, so it was only fitting he met his future wife, Toshimi, at the San Francisco Buddhist temple. Toshimi, who lived in London after leaving her native Nagoya, Japan, was in San Francisco to visit a death-row prisoner with whom she had been corresponding as a means of protesting capital punishment. Toshimi and Fred continued a long-distance relationship between San Francisco and London for more than a year. They married in 1999 in a beautiful castle on the outskirts of London, owned by the Buddhist sect to which they belonged.

The newlyweds lived in Toshimi's tiny London flat for a while, but the bathroom-down-the-hall scenario did not appeal to Fred's American sensibilities. They soon announced they were expecting a baby, and although Toshimi had a difficult pregnancy, I received an exuberant call from Fred ten minutes after Melody Harumi Friedland was born on September 22, 2000, in London. "I can't believe I have a daughter," he said. "She has skin like ice cream." I now treasure the time I spend with my beautiful niece, who is delightful in every way.

Melody, after a student piano recital

Gazelle eventually moved from California to Madison, Wisconsin, where Sarah and Mike were living, and where she met her husband, Jim. They were married in May 1983, in a synagogue, despite Jim's strong Catholic heritage.

Gazelle and Jim in Madison, Wisconsin, 1983

Gazelle and Jim moved to Florida soon after their wedding, and their children, Ari and Timothy, were born there. They now live in Seattle.

Sarah

Just as I grew up holding Sarah in awe, I was in awe of her throughout our lives. She had the self-confidence to undertake major projects and see them through to completion, whether it was starting a new daycare or creating a brand-new hospice facility. She was amazing, and she was my big sister.

While my apartment is always meticulous and even a stray magazine looks out of place, Sarah's entire environment—house, car, office, self—was generally a disorganized, disheveled mess. Once, when she was forced to clean out her car, she actually found a whole chicken rotting under the seats. As a young girl, she always said she was not put on this earth to be a domestic, and she never acted otherwise. Ironically, even around all this clutter, Sarah had an incredibly organized mind and at work she knew where every item was on her desk and what needed to happen. She wasn't a paper pusher; Sarah knew how to deal with people, how to solicit funds, how to delegate.

Outward appearances were not important to her. What was important was caring for other people. In fact the concept of self-lessness was so engrained, she tried to talk me out of a career as a pianist and piano teacher, which was a conversation comparable to one where the participants speak different languages. She couldn't understand the draw I felt, and I couldn't understand how she couldn't see my point of view. We eventually agreed to disagree, and later she accepted my career choice and was ultimately happy it brought me so much satisfaction.

Sarah and her husband didn't want their children to know about her family and background. They wanted to remain as a perfect, insular family, which certainly meant leaving her childhood out of the picture. She continued our family tradition of keeping secrets, and didn't even tell her children the good stuff. I was looking at old photos with Sarah's daughters once and mentioned that she was valedictorian of her high school class. They were shocked to hear this, since their mom had never mentioned it. I found this astonishing, because Sarah's valedictory speech was one of the defining moments of my childhood, as well as of so many City Terrace refugee families. But she never told her children. Was it modesty? Just another family secret? Did Sarah want to shed her early life, the good and the bad, and be done with it?

Even close friends never knew the early history of her life. When asked, she would simply say she was from California and would not relate any of the drama of her early life in Siberia. She generally never told anyone she was Jewish, or about her parents' heartbreaking story. Once, later in life, she told me about meeting a couple on a cruise whose parents were Holocaust survivors. For one of the few times in her life, she discussed her own story and later described how cathartic it was for her.

Two major things defined Sarah's life: her 1960s Berkeley education, which formed her strong, liberal views, and her close family unit—Mike and her two daughters—which she fiercely protected. In the late 1970s, Sarah became interested in the nascent discipline of death and dying. She and Mike were living in Santa Barbara when she became a board member of the then-new concept called a hospice, which first began in the United States in 1974. In 1981, they moved to Madison, and Sarah got a job as director of a hospice. She helped it grow from a basement office into a significant facility, then when the family moved back to California, she went to work for Kaiser Permanente, where she was soon in charge of all the Kaiser hospices in California. Everyone who worked for her adored her, and she adored each of her employees in return.

Around 1993, Sarah moved to Nashville to take a job as executive director of Alive Hospice, but Mike couldn't find a job in Tennessee. Eventually, she moved back to California yet again, and in 1997, became executive director for the Hospice of Napa Valley (HNV). When she started the job, HNV was just a little office, but under her leadership, HNV earned non-profit status, and she established the Adult Day Services of Napa Valley. She began fundraising for a new building and raised $7 million for a new facility.

Sarah was on a number of boards and commissions in California related to hospice care, and she received multiple awards for her innovative work with hospices. She traveled all over the world to consult with hospice organizers. Regrettably, her care and concern for others didn't include taking care of herself. She neglected her health and almost never went to a doctor, until she finally capitulated under extreme prodding from family members. Sarah's good fortune started to run out in 1997 when she was diagnosed with uterine cancer. She had a hysterectomy and discovered that the cancer had spread, but kept working even as she underwent radiation and chemotherapy. She was in remission for three and a half years, until tumors were discovered on her liver. The doctors told her that uterine cancer didn't normally spread to the liver, and they continued to treat her for uterine cancer. A colonoscopy didn't find anything in her colon. Eventually, her pain worsened and she was hospitalized, only to find that she did, in fact, have a tumor on her colon, hidden behind a valve. The Stage 4 colon cancer was spreading voraciously and was the cause of the tumors that metastasized to the liver. She had been treated for the wrong cancer for more than a year.

During the next few years, Sarah refused to submit to the cancer and endured countless surgeries and procedures. It seemed as if every time we spoke, she was having her liver resected or dealing with an infection. She attacked her cancer as she did everything else—with enthusiasm and ambition, without cynicism or bitterness. She loved people and had faith in her doctors and believed she could just keep going, but after nine years of medical misery, Sarah, a survivor of the Holocaust, couldn't survive anymore.

As her health deteriorated, she and I spoke of our early lives as displaced persons, growing up in America as second generation children of Holocaust survivors. Although she barely had the strength to talk on the phone, we spoke about our memories, the good and the bad—the awkwardness of our attempts to assimilate in a new country with parents who were so permanently injured. I couldn't get used to the idea of Sarah being so sick; she had always been a fountain of strength and stability for me.

On the day before she died, I got a call from her husband telling me she didn't have much time. I immediately boarded a plane and flew from Houston to California, only to learn that she had died while I was in flight. Sarah was sixty-three years old. That night I went to dinner with Mike and their daughters, and spent the night in a hotel; in the morning they came to pick me up for breakfast. They said they had already sprinkled Sarah's ashes into the Pacific Ocean. I got on a plane back to Houston, feeling empty and adrift.

I'll always remember her words to me whenever anyone complained about their past. She would say, "It's not important what happened to you in life. What's important is what you do with your life."

Sarah and Ruth, 1951, Los Angeles,
Photo by Mietek

My sister died on June 15, 2006, after a long illness, and I still grieve each day and feel an emptiness I just can't fill. In some ways, I felt closer to Sarah than any other living person. We understood each other so well, we didn't have to speak. We could look at each other and know what the other was thinking. A deep, significant part of me died when she did.

Later that year, Sarah's family and coworkers held a memorial service in the Hospice of Napa Valley, a stately new building she had worked diligently to establish. This was her legacy— even while she was suffering, to lessen the suffering of others; even while she was dying, to ease the process of dying for others.

Chapter 17

PIANO LESSON

A s for me, I continued to play the piano, worked, and earned a bachelor's degree, while Ron and I gradually grew apart. To my puzzlement he became distant and cold soon after we were married. Only a few months later, and before we relocated from Southern California to the Bay Area, I knew in my heart I had made a serious mistake. Not a kernel of the love I had once felt from him existed. And before I was twenty-one, I knew the marriage, with so much strife, was destined to fail. I wanted with all my heart to have a relationship built on mutual respect and love, and although we had shared some happy moments, the longer we were together, the worse the situation became. Slowly, incrementally, the relationship dissolved, and in 1976 we divorced.

In hindsight, I see how dangerous it was to fall so hard for someone at age seventeen, and to marry after only a few months of dating, much of which was carried out long distance through love letters. My mother saw through everything, from beginning to end of my marriage to Ron, but said very little. It was not within her character to be judgmental, but she had met his parents and sternly warned me that ours would be a difficult marriage. I had gone from one unhappy home to another, with conflicts beyond what should normally be the experiences and memories of a young woman.

I thought carefully about where to turn next, and remembered my mother always telling me to follow my dreams and seek a profession I loved. I'd been studying piano again at a Bay Area conservatory, where I was encouraged to become a professional pianist, and so I made the decision to leave my public relations job and get a fresh start. I turned to my lifelong source of refuge—music.

I moved to Vienna to study music and piano performance for nearly two years, and then home to continue my graduate education at Indiana University. To support myself, I got a work-study job in the biology department, which was truly a pleasant break, but which was also where, out of the blue, I fell in love again.

I had met most of the department's faculty, including a kind and handsome assistant professor, Bill Klein. The two of us started dating and getting to know each other. Bill and I developed a strong, intense relationship, but we both needed to clear matters of the heart before we could be sure of our future as a couple. So I decided to give myself distance from him. I left Bloomington and moved to New York City, where music abounded at nearly every corner. New York felt so right to me at the time. I had a day job, first with an architectural firm and then with Orpheus Chamber Orchestra, but was also able to continue my work as a pianist, performing in master classes. I reveled in the rich cultural life in the arts and in music, and had close friendships.

A favorite saying among New Yorkers, however, was that "it's impossible to have a good job, a good apartment, and a good relationship all at the same time in New York City." Bill had moved to Houston where he took a job in the biochemistry department at The University of Texas MD Anderson Cancer Center, and he desperately wanted me to join him there. It made no sense for me to leave New York, yet some nagging inner voice told me I had to give romance one more try. So, with my close friend Julia waving good-bye, and with tears streaming down my face, I got into a cab and rode from my West End apartment to

Penn Station to catch a train to meet Bill in Washington, DC. From there, I was Houston bound. Although my close friends predicted disaster, my choice was based on an innate sense that Bill and I shared many thoughts and values. We had the potential to bring two halves into a whole. It was a decision of the heart, but it didn't make leaving Manhattan any easier.

Our wedding, April 19, 1992, Houston, Texas

After all the chaos of my childhood and young adulthood, after living in twenty-two different cities for the first thirty-seven years of my life, I was no longer a displaced person. I was home.

We were married on April 19, 1992, at Houston's elegant Warwick Hotel. My father came to the wedding, but my mother did not. Curt was ill, so she stayed home to care for him, but she probably also wanted to avoid seeing Daddy, who was genuinely disappointed that Mom had not shown up.

Over the years, my relationship with Bill has deepened. When we first met, we realized how much we enjoyed the rich cultural background of being Jewish, and it turns out that a scientist and a musician are a remarkably great combination. Perhaps this is because we value our commitment to pursuing distinct versions of the truth, free from commercial or partisan interests.

Student piano recital in memory of Sarah, University of St. Thomas, 2006

I was a piano teacher for twenty-three years, but stopped soon after Sarah's death. Our final student recital was dedicated to her memory, and the pieces my students performed were chosen on the basis of music Sarah played when she was young. The last piece in the recital was "Puff the Magic Dragon," a 1960s favorite of hers by Peter, Paul, and Mary. I had the words printed in the program, and while two of my students played, the audience of about 150 people sang along. The last poignant verses tell the story of vanished innocence and the sadness of losing someone close:

> *His head was bent in sorrow; green scales fell like rain;*
> *Puff no longer went to play along the cherry lane.*
> *Without his life-long friend, Puff could not be brave,*
> *So Puff, that mighty dragon, sadly slipped into his cave.*

I loved teaching piano, and recalled the high regard in which I held my piano teachers when I was a child. Bill claims the piano defines me, and he may be right. The piano has been with me no matter where I've lived or what I've done. Being a musician is a rigorous time commitment, but I can't imagine a more fulfilling career or way of living.

My parents went through so much trauma simply because they were born Jews. They lost spouses, children, parents, siblings,

Four hands—Ruth and Shelly (Bill's sister) at my piano studio, 2014

grandparents, and other extended family. They lost wealth. They lost their careers, social standing, and prestige. They lost their Polish homeland and their place in the world. And they were the lucky ones, because they survived. Six million European Jews lost their lives.

After the war, my parents were left with the possibility of a new beginning in a new country, with one child, Sarah, who survived the war, and with their Jewish faith and heritage. But the defining characteristic of my parents—their Jewishness—is what caused them to stand stripped of nearly of all they knew. This was profoundly passed on to me.

Beyond my feelings for Judaism, the most treasured offering my deeply scarred parents left to me was the gift of music and a new piano with the plaque that read: "To Sarah and Ruth with love from Mother and Father." I will always play the piano. Perhaps that plaque explains why.

Although Bronia and Mietek Friedland were too crippled by the past to live as responsible parents for four needy offspring, they were my mother and father. They gave me Sarah first, and then Freddy and Gazelle. And despite their own pain, in their own warped and wounded ways, they gave me life—and buried somewhere within that ravaged gift of life, they gave me love.

Ruth and Sarah, Germany, 1948

Chapter 18

SECOND GENERATION

The idea of writing a memoir about our childhood first came up in a conversation with Sarah not long before her death, on a Sunday evening in late spring, 2006. It was soon after the death of our Uncle Josef, and we spoke about the good and bad memories we had of him and his wife. Sarah came up with the idea: "I think we should write our memoirs. Our upbringing seems so bizarre compared to most people I know. I'd want it to stand out differently than other memoirs . . . in a style unique to our family's history." I agreed with her, and after I hung up the phone, I continued to think about how this could take form. I started reading other memoirs, including those of Holocaust survivors, but found few by second generation survivors.

In my next conversation with Sarah, we spoke about her reunion with old friends from the hospice, a group of six or eight women she knew through work. They had formed very close bonds and would meet every year on Sanibel Island, Florida, and spend about a week together. Sarah always looked forward to these retreats and enjoyed them tremendously, but that spring she was far too ill to travel. So the friends met instead in Oxnard, California—not far from Sarah's home in Santa Barbara, and she raved about what a fantastic time she'd had. She derived such pleasure from her close friendships, so the reunion left her jubilant in spite of being seriously ill. That was the last conversation Sarah and I had.

Now, as I complete her last wish—to write this memoir—I realize what my mother lived with after the war. The word *survivor* has taken on new meaning for me. My mother, who had lost her two sisters, always referred to them when any of her children argued. She reminded us that she had lost her intelligent, beautiful, and talented sisters, so we should cherish our siblings. My mother kept her grief close always—she never overcame the loss of her family to the unspeakable circumstances of Nazi occupation. Her life was tormented by this loss, and even though she had children whom she loved, she always carried this tragedy with her. I have the same grief for my sister and know it will be with me as long as I live. Yet after the anger of losing a sister, the human heart finds its way of coping. In me, I see my mother—and not just her hand coming out of the end of my sleeve. I am more like her now than I ever thought I would be.

All I knew as a child was my family and the other survivor families who lived near us in City Terrace. That was my whole world. As I grew older, however, I began to realize that my childhood was different from that of most American children.

While writing this book about my family, I discovered a myriad of articles, books, doctoral theses, papers, movies, plays, and poems about how survivors and their children have coped with the losses and horrors they experienced. Each person's reaction is unique, based on their inherent characteristics as well as their circumstances. Not surprisingly, I have found that some common denominators hold true for many who, like me, are members of the second generation.

I learned that few survivors ever sought psychological treatment. Perceptions about therapy were different in the post-war years than they are today, and most people believed seeking psychiatric help was a sign of weakness. My father, who clearly needed help, was forced into psychiatric hospitals against his will many times, but once released, he never sought support on his own.

Sarah and Ruth at Long Beach, 1953

Some second generation children, like me, felt they'd been deprived of an unfettered childhood. They describe their childhoods as serious, withdrawn, clutched, and monotone, which are familiar to me; obviously, I was not alone. Children of survivors complain about their parents' emotional unavailability, overprotectiveness, and lack of empathy. Feelings of guilt, anger, depression, mistrust of others, and fear are common among the second generation.

In recent studies, scientists have discovered alterations in the genomes of second generation survivors, so that they share common characteristics passed down from their survivor parents. These alterations are called "epigenetic," but these studies are still unconfirmed. I realized nonetheless how relevant they might be to my own genome! The alterations are called "epigenetic" because they are not stably inherited mutations in the DNA itself, but rather chemical modifications, usually caused by external forces, that are inherently less stable but can nevertheless persist over several generations. The traumas my parents experienced might have influenced my own behavior.

In other words, there may be a scientific basis for these common feelings of displacement and depression and anxiety. The results of these studies are very new and therefore may not be fully understood without further investigation.

Many of the quirks I thought were peculiar to my family can be seen in other Holocaust survivors. My mother definitely fit the frequently described survivor patterns. She was usually kind, she was usually sweet, but she never seemed 100 percent there for her children. I can't blame her now, because I realize she did the best she could with what she had left after a life of fear, struggle, and devastating loss. Emotionally unavailable is exactly how I would describe her.

Other common descriptors for Holocaust-survivor parents are overbearing, intrusive, controlling, and inflexible. This was my father, with a heavy dose of physical and verbal abuse thrown in. Anger is a problem for many survivors, with males displaying much greater rage than females. Some members of the second generation report emotional explosions and other irrational behaviors, just as in my house.

Not every survivor family showed overprotectiveness in the same way. My father's way was to control everything and beat us when situations were not exactly the way he thought they should be. His way was to put a lock on the telephone so he could monitor who and what came in and out of our house. His way was to make a rule that we could not even close the bathroom door. But some families did it differently by making sure their children had everything they wanted or by hovering over them to protect them from all perceived harm, the precursors of "helicopter parents."

These survivors wanted their children to be happy and problem-free, to symbolize all that was lost. Some parents, such as my father, demanded this; some, like my mother, failed to notice (or chose to ignore) issues their children were experiencing, such as being morose, depressed, anxious, or defiant; and some tried to make it happen by shielding and protecting. But *happy* and *problem-free* are not adjectives I would ever use to describe my childhood years.

Two other related themes in my Holocaust research probably should not have surprised me, but did. One was that my parents were not unique in having secrets they kept from their children. Many children of survivors learned as adults for the first time about children and spouses who had died or disappeared, just as Sarah and I found out about her real father, Nathan, after we'd reached adulthood.

The other revelation for me was that at least half the children of survivors know few details about what their parents endured during the war. I generally have a terrific memory, but I recall very little about what my parents said about the war years. As I have been working on this book, I've wondered why I never thought to ask my mother and father more specifics about the Warsaw Ghetto, their time in Siberia, the Russian prison where my father was sent, the relatives they lost. Perhaps I was just too self-absorbed to listen to their stories. Most survivors kept these details from their children even though they felt free to tell others outside the family. Whether it was a desire to shield them from the pain and burden of these experiences or to avoid reliving this pain themselves, I don't know. Most children, like me, did not raise these questions for fear of inflicting further misery on their parents, or because it was simply too harrowing for them to hear about the atrocities and suffering. Thrown in may be a certain amount of the children's self-preservation—their worries about coping with these recollections and how it will affect them. Second generation literature points out that children of survivors generally cannot recall the numbers tattooed on their parents' arms or even which arm the tattoo was on. It may also be that young children are not developmentally ready to ask those questions.

Interestingly, as the survivors and their children age, more conversations are taking place and more children want to know the truth. For me, as for many others, it's too late to find out precisely what our parents endured. Now that my life is in a place where I could handle it, I wish I knew.

Chapter 19

PNINA

Pnina, 1947 (with her husband Grisha, Uncle Josef, and unknown man)

Working on this book produced a totally unexpected development. I discovered a wonderful relative previously unknown to me, and I still have a hard time believing it happened. After my father died, I found among his belongings a small bundle of letters written in Polish. These letters sat in a box for more than a decade before I had them translated. Most were from Josef, after the war, but there was one letter from a name I didn't recognize. It was written in 1976, and the return address was in Tel Aviv. The writer thanked my father for the many holiday gifts he had sent and expressed a wish for him to make a return visit to Israel. There was mention of the wonderful time they'd had celebrating Passover together in 1974, and of hope that the ritual would continue. Also mentioned was my father's new wife, with wishes of happiness in the future.

I thought the writer might be my father's brother-in-law, who was with him on that fateful day when they learned the rest of the family had been shot in the ghetto, and that perhaps he had immigrated to Israel after the war. My father never spoke about him, he never told me of what became of his first wife's brother, and I didn't know his name or if he was still alive.

I contacted the Israeli Ministry of Population Records, whose phone number I'd been given by the Tracing Department of the Holocaust Memorial Museum in Washington, DC, and inquired about Zwi Dunai, the name on the letter. The man in Israel spoke little English (and I do not speak Hebrew), but he was able to tell me that Zwi had died in 1998 and the address changed in 2000. I asked if he had any relatives, but the man hung up on me.

Then I asked an Israeli friend, Reuben Lotan, who was a well-respected scientist in the field of thoracic and head and neck cancer research at MD Anderson to help me search for this person. He got in touch with his niece in Israel, who searched the Tel Aviv white pages under the surname Dunai. She sent me a list of six names and addresses, and I wrote a letter to the person with the most Polish-sounding first name on the list. About two weeks later, I got a call from a social worker at a senior-living residence in Tel Aviv. She was calling on behalf of a resident there who had received my letter but spoke no English. Through the translator I asked if the resident's husband could have been my father's brother-in-law, but she said no, this wasn't possible. The letter recipient was curious as to how I had her address and the former address from 1976 that I had included in the letter. I told her I would send her a copy of the Polish letter from my father's records.

Within two weeks, I got another phone call from the same social worker telling me that Pnina (pronounced Pah-NE-nah) Dunai, the woman I had written to, was my second cousin. Pnina's paternal uncle was my paternal grandfather, therefore she and my father were first cousins. She asked me how old I was, and when I told her I was born in 1947, I heard Pnina yell out in the background, "Rutha!" She remembered me from a visit to Stuttgart when I was an infant. "Evidently, you two need to converse," the social worker said. "Do you speak Hebrew or Polish?"

I said no, but that I speak German and French. When Pnina heard "German," she took the phone and we began our conversations that day. It was April 7, 2009—Pnina's eighty-ninth birthday!

I reported my success to my Israeli friend, who told me of a similar situation that had occurred in his family. He found a relative living in Romania and traveled there to meet her after thinking for most of his life that she had been lost in the war.

I wrote to Pnina, explaining in more detail why I was contacting her and I also sent some family photos. In a few weeks I received a letter back with photos enclosed—one of them of my mother, me as a baby, and a woman who I now know as Pnina. Her real name was Polina, but after the war, when she received new papers, the clerk misspelled it as Pnina, and so it appeared on all her documents.

Pnina, my mother, and me, 1947

The photos she included were identical to the copies I possessed and had sent her; in other words, we both owned the same photographs and sent them to each other. One is a portrait of my father, others were taken in Stuttgart such as the one below. Also included were photos taken when my father visited Tel Aviv in 1974.

My father and Pnina, Germany, 1947

I started to call Pnina regularly, and my rusty German improved as we spoke more often. A widow with no children, she lived alone in the retirement home and was delighted to find some family to combat her loneliness. As many European Jews of her generation, she had lost her whole family during the war.

After a few months she encouraged me to visit her, and although she sounded as if she were in fine health, she kept reminding me she was eighty-nine years old and didn't know how much longer she would be alive. I was excited to meet this mystery relative, so Bill and I planned our first visit to Israel in November 2009.

It was immediately clear when we arrived that Pnina too had been looking forward to our visit. In our hotel room was an abundant arrangement of fresh roses with a card from her to welcome us. I realized during that first meeting that she was now my only connection to my family's past, and similarly, she was curious and excited to meet a surviving relative in person. As I walked toward her along the hallway of her apartment, I was struck by her appearance. Here came a ninety-year-old woman who stood erect, her blonde hair beautifully coifed, dressed in black slacks, a black sweater with thin white bands, and a strand of pearls around her neck, and with just the right amount of makeup. She took my hand in hers, and when she came close to kiss my cheek, she sent forth a slight, tantalizing scent of French perfume. Her hands were soft and smooth and I could feel her warmth and happiness.

She was a bit more reserved than I, since our only conversations until then had been brief phone calls, but the first thing she said was *"Die Augen!"* ("The eyes!"). In my eyes she recognized my family, perhaps reflecting my father's eyes as she remembered them. She was apologetic about her apartment being so small, and told us that after her husband's death, she relocated to this assisted-living building in a northern section of Tel Aviv with a few things from her larger home. I responded by saying, *"Es ist klein aber gemütlich"* ("It is small but cozy"), which must have made her happy, because she repeated it to me, with a touch of humor, in a later phone conversation.

Her table was perfectly laid out with a lace tablecloth, plates of chocolates, and a variety of cakes, fresh grapes, and glass coffee cups with saucers. I sensed she had learned to entertain this way growing up in Poland, and her habits had not changed over the years. She peppered me with questions about my parents, about Uncle Josef and Roselle, and their lives in America. Likewise, I asked about my grandparents, my aunt, the half sister who was killed when she was two years old, and their lives before they were sent to the Warsaw Ghetto. She reflected on her youth and on visiting my grandparents' home on weekends with her older sister, and on how especially kind they were. Pnina and her sister spent a great deal of time in my father's home; they took part in family life and she described clearly, as though it were yesterday, my father's and Josef's characteristics and personalities, their differences and similarities. I asked if they'd had a piano, and she said they did. There was so much I wanted to know.

Pnina in Tel Aviv, 2012

After that visit, I returned to Tel Aviv every year. Pnina was a personal missing link to my past. I hadn't known there still were healthy, happy relatives on my father's side of the family. I learned from Pnina that my father's mental health was fine before 1939; she described him as happily married with one infant and successfully running a large business, taking over the responsibilities of his father. One of my uncle's letters mentions that he was "sensitive" before the war, but there was no indication of emotional or mental disorders.

It was an enormous relief to learn my lineage was not entirely pathological. Until I "discovered" Pnina, the only information I had about my relatives who perished in the war were their photographs, but now I had more details and insights into their lives. She felt it was such a shame that we did not know each other for all those years.

Pnina had a remarkable ability to focus on what truly matters in life and to let the rest go. If something was not going well, she would say to me, *"Nichts zu machen"* ("Nothing to do about it"), even in response to ongoing threats from suicide bombers and rockets launched by enemies of Israel. One of her favorite mottoes was: "Why worry?" Each encounter brought us closer together and more comfortable talking about the past. As with all survivors, volumes could be written about her experience of the war—the hardships of cold and hunger, and the loss of loved ones, especially the pain of losing children. And because others should not forget, here is her story:

Pnina grew up in Chelm, a town near Poland's eastern border, about 160 miles from Warsaw. She met her husband, Grisha, in 1938 while she was a student and living in Warsaw with her only sister. She and Grisha were deeply in love, but were separated in 1939 by the German invasion conquering the western half of Poland. Grisha's family lived on the Soviet side of the country, in Kowel. His parents wrote a letter to her parents asking if they would send a servant to bring Pnina to him so they could be married. Her parents agreed, and Pnina left her family, carrying a rucksack on her back. She never dreamed it would be the last time she saw them.

Pnina and Grisha were married in his home on November 11, 1939, under a *chuppa*, the traditional four-poster canopy used to shelter the bride and groom at Jewish weddings.

Pnina's sister, Felah, joined them in Kowel, where they all lived with Grisha's parents. A few weeks later, German soldiers flushed out all the Jews in Chelm and forced them to walk to Russia. Those who couldn't go by foot were shot. Pnina's father, she later learned, was shot on the first night of Hanukkah, just shortly after her wedding.

Pnina and Grisha escaped from Poland to Ukraine, and she found herself at a train station once again carrying all her possessions in a rucksack. All the train stations had become human stockyards, layered in filth and excrement, with people crowding and searching for someplace to sit while waiting for a train or for information that might help them escape. The stations became more frenetic every day, hour by hour. Tuberculosis, typhus, dysentery, cholera, diphtheria, and scarlet fever ravaged the terminals and spread between passengers and refugees living under appalling, unsanitary conditions.

Hordes of men, women, and children were trying to leave at the same time. Because they had no destination and no time schedules for reference, Pnina explained, if people saw an open door, they got in. They took a gamble on where they would be taken.

She and her husband boarded a train, thinking and hoping it was going east, but having no idea where it would make its stops. When they reached Stalingrad, they got off the train holding on to their few belongings. Together with so many Jews and other Europeans who had been abruptly rendered homeless, they moved on, arriving first in Tashkent. There they found work, and for three years lived in a small city nearby through freezing winters, in the barest quarters with scant food. Pnina gave birth to a daughter, Lena, but the baby succumbed to the merciless conditions and died in the night. Pnina and Grisha buried Lena somewhere in the woods. With only white fields of snow for a landmark, Pnina was never able to find where her little girl's grave was. Decades later, when she spoke of the loss of her child, she still trembled from unfathomable sorrow.

In 1944, Pnina and Grisha followed the Russian troops back to Poland with their rucksacks on their backs and no visas, only to learn that their parents and siblings had been murdered by the Nazis. In the months that followed, they made many efforts to reach Palestine. In one attempt to cross the Pyrenees Mountains, they followed a group of Greeks who seemed to know how to reach a place of safety. At the border, the guard kept asking Pnina if she was Greek, but she said nothing. He continued to taunt, and she refused to speak. Finally he yielded, saying to her, "if you are a Grecian, then I am a Martian," and he let her through.

Pnina and Grisha wandered from one country to another, along with many refugees, determined to reach Palestine. Because they were applying for immigration, they wound up in a displaced-persons camp in Munich, where she learned that my father was alive in a camp in Stuttgart. She and her husband traveled there to see him, his new wife, and Sarah and me. During this time they also made the trip to Brussels to see Josef. It was a joyous reunion for them, and they remained in contact for the rest of their lives, though my father's new family was never relevant in their communications. When I think about it now, I realize that they related on the basis of the years before the war.

Finally, in November 1948, Pnina and Grisha reached Israel. The country was in shambles, torn by war with various neighboring Arab countries; still, they felt this would now be their home. With "their ten fingers each," they rebuilt their lives and their new country. At first they lived in what is now called Old Tel Aviv, Neve Tzedik, in the southwestern section of the city, the first Jewish neighborhood built outside the walls of the ancient port of Jaffa. Pnina walked long distances back and forth to work, but as life improved in the new nation, they moved to a new neighborhood, surrounded by interesting architecture, the symphony hall, art museums, shops, and the leafy tree-lined Rothschild Boulevard and King George Street. They watched the newly planted trees and seedlings grow to full size, bringing lushness and shade to otherwise sun-drenched streets.

It was mysterious to Pnina and me why my father never mentioned any of this, particularly since we grew up thinking we had no living relatives. Sarah and I were terribly saddened to believe we were all that was left of the Friedland family, and my father could have easily corrected this misconception.

Pnina did not have any family photographs from the 1930s— none of my grandmother Malka; of Josef and his wife, Eva; of his sister, Aunt Genia; or of my father's first wife, Junia, and their daughter, whose name I do not know. But she recognized everyone in the photos—some taken by my father with his Leica. All of these photos had been precious to me in my childhood and in my possession since my father's death. I made a family album beginning with all these early photographs—of my mother, her family, my siblings, and also their children, loved ones, and friends. But the ones of Sarah meant much to me. I wanted her children to have them as well, hopefully to pass on and keep the stories embedded within them alive.

When Pnina read the affectionate letters written between 1945 and 1954 from Josef to my father, she was especially troubled by their subsequent estrangement, given the emotion, sentimentality, and love expressed in them. I tried to avoid talking about my father's mental health and decline. She knew what a difficult time Mietek had in America—that he was a failure in supporting his family, which was unconscionable to her. She wanted to know why Josef did not help my father.

I had difficulty explaining the complexity of my immediate family, but Pnina was sharp and quickly read between the lines when I described their sadness and difficulty communicating. I intentionally left out the jealousy, paranoia, and violence.

Uncle Josef

She was careful when speaking about my mother. My father had told her that my mother had left him and taken the children away because another man could give her a better life. I tried to clarify the facts and explain how contorted his view was. It was a challenge for me to express the true sentiment of my mother without damaging Pnina's image of my father.

Pnina and her husband had lived through their own horrors, but the difference was that they truly loved each other from the beginning to the end. This is not the case for many survivors, some of whom dashed into marriages still numb from grief and anguish. Some were fortunate and found lasting relationships and remained in love for decades. Cesia Kingston once told me that she married soon after the war, and that a friend named Hanka, who was also getting married, knew so little about her future husband she couldn't even remember his name. As it turned out, the couple eventually immigrated to America, continued their friendship with Cesia and Morrie, and remained married for sixty-three years! Pnina and Grisha were also a couple whose love never diminished or weakened during their sixty years together.

$$\sim$$

Pnina's training before the war led her to a job in the Israeli Ministry of Education, where she became a leader in ORT (an education and vocational training organization). Her husband's career was with the department of transportation, where he worked as a statistician until his early retirement due to a heart condition. Rather than leave him home alone, Pnina retired earlier too, and their lives became even fuller. They took long walks in their neighborhood, enjoyed concerts at the Tel Aviv Performing Arts Center, and went often to the Tel Aviv Museum of Art. They spent time with close friends and, during the hot summer months, at least a month in a summerhouse on the outskirts of Frankfurt. They traveled throughout Europe and made new and lasting friendships.

Pnina reminisced fondly about how Grisha dressed in a suit and tie every day. His colleagues would ask if he was going to a bar mitzvah. She continued to refer to him as Grisha, even though Grisha Duvaniwski became Zwi Dunai after they moved to Israel. Although they mastered Hebrew, Pnina and Grisha continued to communicate with each other in Polish.

After his death in 1998, Pnina felt lost and alone. Gradually, her friends did not visit as much, and she was grieving for and missing her husband. She went out early in the morning for her newspapers, ran a few errands, and by noon was home again. Her only contacts were by telephone or with her housekeeper, who urged her to consider senior housing, and finally Pnina took her advice. She celebrated her eightieth birthday in this new environment, and some of her old friends came to visit, but gradually the people from the past disappeared and her circle was reduced to "Little Tel Aviv," the name of this home for the elderly.

Pnina learned how to play bridge in these later years of her life, something similar to breathing fresh air, she explained.

Thinking, using her mind, and being with people, without being obligated to make small talk, made her happy. She enjoyed the many activities arranged by the staff at the assisted-living apartment, including theater, concerts, lectures, and festivities for the holidays. As did many people in Israel, she lived a secular life, although she enjoyed the Jewish traditions and holidays.

～

Israel is one of the world's most beautiful countries, but I was not prepared for the new emotions I felt on my visits there. It holds the profound spirit of my ancestry, and whether they are secular or religious, its citizens are well versed in the history of Jewish people. I sense that the very existence of the citizens depends on this history. Music and science are practiced at the highest level, as is education. On Holocaust Day—Yom Hashanah, on the twenty-seventh day of Nisan (April/May) on the Jewish calendar—every thirteen-year-old goes on a field trip with his or her teachers to see monuments and museums dedicated to Holocaust victims and heroes. During Yad Vashem they commemorate the six million Jews who died under Nazi occupation. Children also learn the history of the Third Reich, how it came to power, and the unfathomable devastation it wrought. At 10:00 a.m. on Yom Hashanah, sirens sound throughout Israel for two minutes, and all citizens stop what they are doing to pay silent tribute to the dead.

～

I spoke with Pnina nearly every Sunday at 7:00 p.m., Tel Aviv time, from the day our lives came together. The occasions when I did not, turned nearly catastrophic. On one Sunday in 2013, I called her and the phone rang repeatedly with no answer. Finally I called the lobby desk and learned that she had lost her footing while getting into a taxicab earlier in the week and had broken her leg. The taxi driver had taken her to the hospital. When I called the hospital hoping to speak to her, the nurse answering the phone asked, "Which cousin are you? The one in Jerusalem or in Tel Aviv?" I was caught off guard, since I didn't realize she had other living relatives, so I simply answered, "The one from America." It was a month before Pnina could return home from the hospital.

On my next trip, I asked about her cousins in Jerusalem and Tel Aviv. She told me she had another uncle who had left Poland and moved to Brazil. His son, who moved to Israel as a young man and settled in Jerusalem, had a career in pharmaceuticals and now had grown children. Because Pnina and I shared the same great-grandparents, I asked her if I was related to him, and she said yes. Why had I never been told I had relatives in South America? She could not answer this question, which was really no different than my asking why I'd never been told I had a second cousin named Pnina living in Israel. That same week on a late Friday afternoon, the widow of Pnina's cousin from Jerusalem called to wish her a *Shabbat shalom*—a good Sabbath.

⁂

Some of my happiest moments in Tel Aviv were in Pnina's apartment eating strawberries and drinking Nescafé. We sat by an open window in the spring breeze, listening to the sounds of birds and children playing in the park just outside the house. In the fall she served us delicious clementines, which I tried to eat as slowly as possible because they were so good.

On one of those days, Bill asked her how old her grandparents had been when they died. She told us her grandfather was 101 years old, which bode well for her own long life. I wondered where he'd been to have survived the war, but I could see this discussion was a strain on her. During her ninety-fourth year, when her health was declining, Bill and I brought her flowers and celebrated Shabbat by lighting the candles and saying the blessings. I recited them and Bill sang responsively. Pnina sang along with him. We used her mother's silver candelabra that she somehow managed to keep throughout the war. Her eyes gleamed when we held this little ritual every Friday. She adored Bill, who teased her and made her smile.

⁂

I still remember some words and phrases in Polish, but very few. Although my parents spoke only in Polish to each other, they never spoke words of endearment. So I must have learned what I said to Pnina as I was leaving her apartment from other Polish-speaking friends, or perhaps from the *Carmen* lyrics that my mother sang to me so long ago. I said softly, "*Ja ciebie Kocham*" ("I love you"). She answered, "*Ja Kocham cie, tez*" ("I love you, too").

In June 2014, Bill and I traveled to Jerusalem to attend the bar mitzvah of Marylin Kingston's youngest son, Shane. It was held at the Hebrew Union College courtyard and a reception followed at the King David Hotel. We were thrilled to celebrate the occasion, and I gave a short talk about the history of our families and how we met as refugees in City Terrace. The bonds we had created then were carried into the third generation.

We drove to Tel Aviv the following day to visit Pnina, who was anxiously awaiting our arrival. She was in good spirits, perhaps a bit more fragile than when we last saw her, but still looked strong and healthy. We told her our news of Bill's sabbatical leave from the University of Texas to relocate as a visiting professor at the Sackler School of Medicine at Tel Aviv University, and she was overjoyed to hear of our living in Tel Aviv.

But when we arrived for this term, I was shocked to see how much her health had declined. She had a twenty-four-hour live-in caregiver, because she could no longer do anything for herself. She had stopped eating and drinking nearly altogether, although everyone made an effort to help her. She also had stopped playing bridge, something she loved to do.

We visited Pnina routinely, either for lunch or afternoon visits, and never missed a Shabbat evening, even when she was too ill to get out of bed. We would celebrate Shabbat in her bedroom, and then carry the candelabra into the living room where she could still see the lights. I brought a fresh bouquet of flowers each Friday and she would look at them with joy, even noticing that sometimes I had glitter sprinkled on the roses. One afternoon, as we were leaving, I asked her if there was something I could bring next time. Her immediate request was for Chanel

No. 5! The next day I arrived with a gift-wrapped package of her favorite perfume. The smile on her face was worth every cent.

Pnina's body had begun to shut down and she was briefly hospitalized for kidney failure. Our conversations went from hours on end when we first met in 2009 to five minutes or less in 2014. She refused to accept herself as an invalid and would not allow me to do anything for her, not even make a cup of coffee or put away a dish. Her table was always set with the finest linen with embroidered edges, fresh chocolates in a crystal bowl, and various sweets and fruits for our enjoyment, no matter how bad she was feeling.

On several occasions she slept from exhaustion while Bill and I stayed with her. Every twenty or thirty minutes she would waken and have a little smile of recognition. Her mind was as sharp as ever. She could recall every detail of her days past and present.

During this time I studied the final work by Schubert for the piano, Sonata in B-Flat, D. 960. The last three of Schubert's sonatas were written during his last months of life and are among the most important of his mature masterpieces. I'd previously played them, but now was savoring this last one in B-flat more than any of the others. For me, it has not only great emotional depth, but also some of Schubert's loveliest and most expressive themes. It also has personal significance as a reminder of my months in Israel and the treasured time I had with Pnina.

She died on February 11, 2015. I received a phone call at 7:15 the following morning from her physiotherapist, who gave me the terrible news and told me that the funeral was set for the following day at 11:00 a.m. I met him then at Pnina's home and we went to the cemetery for the burial.

I had never been to a funeral in Israel, but soon learned that if you are Jewish, an Orthodox burial is the only choice available. The first order of business was for a blood relative to identify the body, and as it happened, that was me. The rabbi removed layers of cloth from the shroud around her head, and I stared into her face, which by then had a greenish pallor. Her mouth was wide open and contorted. I felt faint at seeing her in this way, just days after being with her in her bedroom, her eyes sparkling. Though she'd been too weak to speak at length, I had no idea she was so close to death.

The day was gray, damp, and cold when I followed the ten Orthodox males dressed in black attire to the gravesite. They began digging through the earth just next to the tombstone of Pnina's husband. They shoveled and shoveled for the longest time, chanting prayers in Hebrew I could not understand. Finally, her small-framed body was covered with a black satin cloth and carried on a stretcher (no coffin) and slipped into the earth. The women present were not allowed to participate, according to tradition, except to place a stone in the grave. Her therapist, Israel, handed me a bouquet of flowers and I set it on her grave along with a handful of earth. I was able to say the *Kaddish*, the Hebrew prayer for the dead so familiar to me from having recited it many times for my parents and sister, but I was shaking and shivering the entire time. The burial took place so swiftly after Pnina's death that Bill could not arrange to be at the funeral.

Israel drove me home, where I sat sobbing, cold, and alone. Countless times I have read, "Life is a journey and death is its destination," but it never lessens the pain. If we survivors of survivors have learned anything, it's to dwell not on what we've lost but on what we have. Pnina enriched my life in so many ways, giving me deep insights into my lost family history while offering unconditional love, comfort, and friendship. She will always be in my heart, and it will be my personal mission to keep her memory—and the memory of millions of others—alive in a world where the past is often hidden or forgotten.

Ruth and Sarah, Jessica and Diane, 1950, Photo by Mietek.

Acknowledgments

Much of the research on which this memoir is based was carried out at the United States Holocaust Memorial Museum, Washington, DC. Important aspects of the story are based on allied research from the International Tracing Service at Bad Arolsen Holocaust archives, International Services of the American Red Cross, Yad Vashem, Remembrance Center and Central Database of Shoah Victims, Holocaust Museum Houston, and last but not least, on contributions from survivors of the Holocaust: their personal experiences both told and written in testimonials and memoirs. I am extremely grateful to all my friends, relatives, and colleagues on this project without whose contributions over the past decade and a half this book would have been impossible. A most special thanks belongs to Judi Shur, my friend and colleague whose input was invaluable, often pointing me in the right direction and encouraging me to tell my story. Thanks, Judi. Viktoria Cseh and Lisa A. DuBois are the editors. Most of the historical photography is by Michael (Mietek) Friedland.

With deep affection and gratitude to my lifelong friends, Bella Stern and Marylin Kingston, and to my husband, Bill Klein.

References

Ahonen, Pertti, Gustave Corni, Jerzy Kochanowski, Rainer Schulze, Tamas Stark, Barbara Stetzl-Marx. *People on the Move, Forced Population Movements in Europe in the Second World* War *and Its Aftermath.* New York: Berg Publishers, 2008.

Congressional Record. Hon. Mile Thompson. *Recognizing Sarah Gorodezky of Napa Valley.* May 2, 2005.

Epstein, Helen. *Children of the Holocaust.* Penguin Books, 1988.

Friedlander, Saul. *When Memory Comes.* Madison, Wisconsin: University of Wisconsin Press, 1979.

Friedlander, Saul. *The Years of Extermination—Nazi Germany and the Jews 1939–1945.* New York: HarperCollins Publishers, 2007.

Gigliotti, Simone and Berel Lang, ed. *The Holocaust, A Reader.* Moscow, Russia: Committee of the Memorial Society, 2006.

Hass, Aaron. *In the Shadow of the Holocaust, The Second Generation.* Cambridge University Press, 1996.

The Holocaust Museum Library. Testimonies. Houston, Texas.

International American Red Cross. Tracing Service. Baltimore, Maryland, and Houston, Texas.

International Tracing Service. Bad Arolsen, Germany.

Jewish Virtual Library. *Oneg Shabbat, the Jewish Underground Archives in the Warsaw Ghetto.*

Konigseder, Angelika and Juliane Wetzel. *Waiting for Hope: Jewish Displaced Persons in Post-World War II Germany.* Northwestern University, 2001.

Levi, Primo. *The Periodic Table.* New York: Shocken Books, 1984.

Levi, Primo. *Survival in Auschwitz.* New York: Simon and Schuster, 1958.

Levine, Renee. *One-Way Tickets.* New York: Eloquent Books, AEG Publishing Group, 2009.

Mendelsohn, Daniel. *The Lost.* New York: HarperCollins Publishers, 2006.

Saved by Deportation. Documentary film. 2007.

ABOUT THE AUTHOR

Ruth Klein was born in Berlin, Germany, and arrived in America as a three-year-old with her parents and older sister. Ruth grew up in Southern California and later moved to Berkeley and the San Francisco Bay Area. Since early childhood, her training in classical music has been the focal point of her life. Growing up surrounded by the history of the Holocaust, she and her sister developed a keen understanding of the impact of the Holocaust on the world. This background led Ruth to formalize her experiences by writing a memoir. Ruth Klein is currently living in Houston, Texas, with her husband, a biomedical scientist. She taught piano in Houston for twenty-three years. Her other interests include the fine arts, literature, and foreign languages.

Ruth Klein is grateful to the organizations such as the United States Holocaust Memorial Museum, Yad Vashem, the International American Red Cross, and the many other worldwide agencies that continually research the Holocaust. Those that trace its victims help alleviate the emotional, spiritual, and psychological distress of survivors and their families by enabling them with information about missing loved ones and documentation, and in some cases reuniting families separated during WWII.

Author photo © Scott Collier

Selected Titles From She Writes Press

She Writes Press is an independent publishing company founded to serve women writers everywhere. Visit us at www.shewritespress.com.

Jumping Over Shadows: A Memoir by Annette Gendler. $16.95, 978-1-63152-170-6. Like her great-aunt Resi, Annette Gendler, a German, fell in love with a Jewish man—but unlike her aunt, whose marriage was destroyed by "the Nazi times," Gendler found a way to make her impossible love survive.

The Coconut Latitudes: Secrets, Storms, and Survival in the Caribbean by Rita Gardner. $16.95, 978-1-63152-901-6. A haunting, lyrical memoir about a dysfunctional family's experiences in a reality far from the envisioned Eden—and the terrible cost of keeping secrets.

Raising Myself: A Memoir of Neglect, Shame, and Growing Up Too Soon by Beverly Engel. $16.95, 978-1-63152-367-0. A powerfully inspiring and unflinchingly honest story of how best-selling author and abuse recovery expert Beverly Engel made her way in the world—in spite of her mother's neglect and constant criticism, undergoing sexual abuse at nine, and being raped at twelve.

Don't Call Me Mother: A Daughter's Journey from Abandonment to Forgiveness by Linda Joy Myers. $16.95, 978-1-938314-02-5. Linda Joy Myers's story of how she transcended the prisons of her childhood by seeking—and offering—forgiveness for her family's sins.

Scattering Ashes: A Memoir of Letting Go by Joan Rough. $16.95, 978-1-63152-095-2. A daughter's chronicle of what happens when she invites her alcoholic and emotionally abusive mother to move in with her in hopes of helping her through the final stages of life—and her dream of mending their tattered relationship fails miserably.

Baffled by Love: Stories of the Lasting Impact of Childhood Trauma Inflicted by Loved Ones by Laurie Kahn. $16.95, 978-1631522260. For three decades, Laurie Kahn has treated clients who were abused as children—people who were injured by someone who professed to love them. Here, she shares stories from her own rocky childhood along with those of her clients, weaving a textured tale of the all-too-human search for the "good kind of love."

CPSIA information can be obtained
at www.ICGtesting.com
Printed in the USA
JSHW011018270920
8263JS00005B/20